SCIENTIFIC AMERICAN EXPLORES BIG IDEAS

Confronting Racism

The Editors of *Scientific American*

SCIENTIFIC AMERICAN EDUCATIONAL PUBLISHING

New York

Published in 2023 by Scientific American Educational Publishing
in association with **The Rosen Publishing Group**
29 East 21st Street, New York, NY 10010

Contains material from Scientific American®, a division of Springer Nature America, Inc., reprinted by permission, as well as original material from The Rosen Publishing Group®.

Copyright © 2023 Scientific American® and The Rosen Publishing Group®.

All rights reserved.

First Edition

Scientific American
Lisa Pallatroni: Project Editor

Rosen Publishing
Joseph Kampff: Compiling Editor
Michael Moy: Senior Graphic Designer

Cataloging-in-Publication Data
Names: Scientific American, Inc.
Title: Confronting racism / edited by the Editors of Scientific American.
Description: New York : Scientific American Educational Publishing, 2023. | Series: Scientific American explores big ideas | Includes glossary and index.
Identifiers: ISBN 9781684169450 (pbk.) | ISBN 9781684169467 (library bound) | ISBN 9781684169474 (ebook)
Subjects: LCSH: Race discrimination–United States–Juvenile literature. | Racism–United States–Juvenile literature. | United States–Race relations–Juvenile literature.
Classification: LCC E184.A1 C664 2023 | DDC 305.800973–dc23

Manufactured in the United States of America
Websites listed were live at the time of publication.

Cover: Angelina Bambina/Shutterstock.com

CPSIA Compliance Information: Batch #SACS23.
For further information, contact Rosen Publishing at 1-800-237-9932.

CONTENTS

Introduction — 5

Section 1: Racism, Prejudice and Implicit Bias — 7

1.1 The Concept of "Race" Is a Lie — 8
By Peter G. Prontzos

1.2 Buried Prejudice: The Bigot in Your Brain — 12
By Siri Carpenter

1.3 How to Think About Implicit Bias — 23
By Keith Payne, Laura Niemi and John M. Doris

1.4 The Flexibility of Racial Bias — 26
By Mina Cikara and Jay Van Bavel

1.5 Microaggressions: Death by a Thousand Cuts — 33
By Derald Wing Sue

Section 2: Racism in Health and Psychology — 37

2.1 Inequality Before Birth Contributes to Health Inequality in Adults — 38
By Janet Currie

2.2 How Doctors Can Confront Racial Bias in Medicine — 51
By Rachel Pearson

2.3 To Achieve Mental Health Equity, Dismantle Social Injustice — 54
By Ruth S. Shim and Sarah Y. Vinson

2.4 Why Racism, Not Race, Is a Risk Factor for Dying of COVID-19 — 59
By Claudia Wallis

2.5 Teaching Antiracism to the Next Generation of Doctors — 64
By Rupinder Kaur Legha

Section 3: Policing Race — 69

3.1 A Civil Rights Expert Explains the Social Science of Police Racism — 70
By Lydia Denworth and Alexis J. Hoag

3.2 How to Reduce Police Violence — 76
By Dina Fine Maron

3.3 Police Violence Calls for Measures Beyond De-Escalation Training — 81
By Stacey McKenna

3.4 I Can't Breathe: Asthma, Black Men and the Police — 86
By Obasi Okorie, Ekemini Hogan and Utibe Effiong

Section 4: Race, Education and Achievement — 89

4.1 Teaching About Racism Is Essential for Education — 90
By the Editors of *Scientific American*

4.2 Where Are the Black Women in STEM Leadership? — 93
By Erika Jefferson

4.3 This Is What the Race Gap in Academia Looks Like — 97
By Amanda Montañez

4.4 The Brilliance Paradox: What Really Keeps Women and Minorities from Excelling in Academia — 99
By Andrei Cimpian and Sarah-Jane Leslie

Section 5: Racism in Science and Technology — 109

5.1 Silence Is Never Neutral; Neither Is Science — 110
By 500 Women Scientists Leadership

5.2 How to Study Racial Disparities — 114
By Bryan Schonfeld and Sam Winter-Levy

5.3 Black Images Matter: How Cameras Helped, and Sometimes Harmed, Black People — 120
By Ainissa G. Ramirez

5.4 The Racist Legacy of Computer-Generated Humans — 124
By Theodore Kim

Section 6: Overcoming Racism — 127

6.1 How to Unlearn Racism — 128
By Abigail Libers

6.2 Charles Blow Tells You How to Actually Fight Racism — 139
By Bernadette Bynoe

6.3 To Fight Bias, Consider Highlighting Your Race or Gender — 146
By Erika Kirgios, Aneesh Rai, Edward Chang and Katy Milkman

6.4 We'll Never Fix Systemic Racism by Being Polite — 150
By Aldon Morris

Glossary — 154
Further Information — 156
Citations — 157
Index — 158

INTRODUCTION

Race and racism are slippery concepts. At its most basic, race is simply a bad idea from the 18th century: that humans can be divided into groups based on physical traits that come down through a shared ancestry. Science, at the time, mobilized to support this idea. Racism is the preference for or belief in the superiority of members of one's own race over members of other races.

But 20th-century advances in genetics would seem to have put the 18th-century concept of race to bed: human beings share 99.99 percent of their genetic material. And with the major gains of the American abolitionist movement of the 19th century and the civil rights movement of the 20th century, culminating in the election of Barack Obama to the presidency of the United States, some came to believe that we are living in a "post-racial society." For a moment, it was possible for some people to believe that race isn't real and that racism is a backward ideology that's on its way out.

This story of race and racism is, of course, an oversimplification. As anyone who's read the papers, seen a movie or TV show, or scrolled through a Twitter feed recently knows, race and racism persist in all their ugliness. Perhaps the most shocking instances of contemporary racism at work are the killings of unarmed Black men—notably Michael Brown and Eric Garner—by white police officers in the 2010s, which brought the Black Lives Matter movement into the national spotlight. Race and the devasting effects of racism are real indeed.

Confronting Racism brings together recent *Scientific American* articles that use science to help untangle the complicated concepts of race and racism, to understand their effects on individuals and society, and, ultimately, to point the way toward creating a less racist society. Section 1, "Racism, Prejudice and Implicit Bias," offers insight into the psychological and linguistic roots of racism. Section 2, "Racism in Health and Psychology," looks at the effects of race and racism on health care and mental health care. Section 3,

"Policing Race," addresses the urgent problems of race and racism as they affect policing and the disproportionate killing of Black males. Section 4, "Race, Education and Achievement," examines the contemporary racial disparities in education and achievement. Questions about how to think about race and racism scientifically and the relationship between race and racism in modern technology are addressed in Section 5, "Racism in Science and Technology." And Section 6, "Overcoming Racism," suggests practical ways to confront and to overcome racism in our day-to-day lives.

Section 1: Racism, Prejudice and Implicit Bias

1.1　The Concept of "Race" Is a Lie
　　　By Peter G. Prontzos

1.2　Buried Prejudice: The Bigot in Your Brain
　　　By Siri Carpenter

1.3　How to Think About Implicit Bias
　　　By Keith Payne, Laura Niemi and John M. Doris

1.4　The Flexibility of Racial Bias
　　　By Mina Cikara and Jay Van Bavel

1.5　Microaggressions: Death by a Thousand Cuts
　　　By Derald Wing Sue

The Concept of "Race" Is a Lie

By Peter G. Prontzos

The plague of racism has, in many ways, been increasing in the last few years. Whether one looks at Hungary, Germany, Myanmar, India or Brazil, racists are becoming more visible and getting elected to public office.

Then there were the horrors of the slaughters in New Zealand and Sri Lanka.

In the United States, the president has denounced Mexicans as drug dealers and rapists, described some poor nations as "shithole countries," and failed to reject an endorsement from a former leader of the Ku Klux Klan. He even went so far as to call at least some neo-Nazis "very fine people." One might be forgiven for thinking that what his campaign slogan really meant was "Make America White Again."

Hate crimes in the U.S. rose in 2017 for the third consecutive year, and they are increasing in Canada too—up 47 percent in the latter in 2017, primarily targeting Muslims but also attacking Jews and people of color.

In combating this increase in racism, there are two primary aspects to consider. The first is that the very idea of "race" is a lie: as the American Society of Human Genetics, the largest professional organization of scientists in the field, explained in an essay:

"The science of genetics demonstrates that humans cannot be divided into biologically distinct subcategories"; and it "challenges the traditional concept of different races of humans as biologically separate and distinct. This is validated by many decades of research." In other words, "race itself is a social construct," with no biological basis.

In 2014, more than 130 leading population geneticists condemned the idea that genetic differences account for the economic, political, social and behavioral diversity around the world. In fact, said a 2018 article in *Scientific American*, there is a "broad scientific consensus that when it comes to genes there is just as much diversity within racial and ethnic groups as there is across them." And the Human Genome Project has confirmed that the genomes found around the globe are 99.9 percent identical in every person. Hence, the very idea of different "races" is nonsense.

A second problem, as cognitive scientist George Lakoff has shown, is that simply using the word "race," even when criticizing racism, actually reinforces the false belief that human beings belong to fundamentally different groups. That's because the more a word is used, the more that certain brain circuits are activated and the stronger that metaphor becomes.

The use of colors to describe ethnic groups also supports racism. That's why it is not acceptable anymore to refer to Asians as "yellow," to Latin Americans as "brown," or to Native Americans as "red." However, many people, including academics and journalists, still use "black" to describe people of primarily recent African origin.

Of course, there are minor differences between various ethnic groups: behavioral, physical, linguistic and so on, and most of those differences are due to one's culture and experiences. As Einstein observed, "the personality that finally emerges is largely formed by the environment" that people experience during development, by the structure of the society in which they grow up, "by the tradition of that society, and by its appraisal of particular types of behavior."

In fact, the idea that all of humanity can be divided into four or five (or however many) racial groups is relatively new. Ancient Greeks, for example, never thought of themselves as "white." As Tim Whitmarsh noted in *Aeon* in 2018, "Greeks simply didn't think of the world as starkly divided along racial lines into black and white: that's a strange aberration of the modern, Western world, a product of many different historical forces, but in particular the transatlantic slave trade and the cruder aspects of 19th-century racial theory."

The truth is that Greek legends portray themselves and their heroes as multiethnic in origin. The Egyptian Danaus became king of Argos, and his daughter, Hypermestra, was an ancestor of the greatest of all Greek heroes, Herakles (Hercules). Perseus, who slew the Gorgon Medusa, married an Ethiopian woman, Andromeda, and their children established the most powerful of all the Bronze Age Greek kingdoms, Mycenae.

Another example of this nonracial perspective is found in the *Histories* of Herodotus, who, in the 5th century B.C., wrote that the purpose of his book was to "preserve the fame of the important and remarkable achievements produced by both Greeks and *non-Greeks*" [emphasis added]. The so-called Father of History also said that Ethiopians "are reputed to be the tallest and most beautiful of all peoples."

This portrait of Africans is not unique. Historian Peter Farb notes in his 1978 book *Humankind* that "Greek art, literature, and mythology often portrayed dark-skinned people with respect." And then there are the remains found in a cave in Cheddar Gorge in southwest England of the individual known as "Cheddar Man." DNA from his skeleton, dated to around 7,100 B.C., suggests that he had blue eyes, dark curly hair and "dark to black" skin pigmentation. Cheddar Man shares a genetic profile with several other individuals found in Spain, Hungary and Luxembourg.

Cheddar Man's forebears likely originated in the Middle East. Later, the ancestors of the people who built Stonehenge traveled west across the Mediterranean from Asia Minor, bringing farming with them and reaching Britain about 4,000 B.C.

The truth is that we are all one human family that had its origins in Africa. Amazingly, research by statistician Joseph Chang at Yale found that the most recent common ancestor of everyone alive today lived just 3,600 years ago. In other words, if you could trace your ancestry back less than 150 generations, you would find at least one person who is the father or mother of us all. And the further back in time one looks, the more common ancestors we would find. Chang concludes:

"Our findings suggest a remarkable proposition: no matter the languages we speak or the color of our skin, we share ancestors who planted rice on the banks of the Yangtze, who first domesticated horses on the steppes of the Ukraine, who hunted giant sloths in the forests of North and South America, and who labored to build the Great Pyramid of Khufu."

The burden of proof lies, therefore, with those who cling to the notion that there are such things as "races." They would have to first provide a scientific definition, based on significant differences in human genomes, of what "race" means; and second, clearly demonstrate that there are enough of these differences between different ethnic groups to justify dividing people into separate "races." This is an impossible task.

In the final analysis, it is our experiences and our culture, not our DNA, that account for most of our differences.

So, while ethnicity is real, and there are indeed minor differences between ethnic groups, there is no such thing as "race"—only racism. And the consequences of racism—from the slave trade to the European genocide of First Nations in the "New World" to Nazi Germany to today's refugees—are horrific.

Even Ronald Reagan understood that, "if suddenly there was a threat to this world from some other species, from another planet," the consequence would be this: "We'd forget all the little local differences that we have between our countries, and we would find out once and for all that we really are all human beings here on this Earth together."

We are facing real existential threats, and we shouldn't wait for an alien invasion before we focus less on our minor differences and more on what we all have in common.

About the Author

Peter G. Prontzos is professor emeritus of political science and interdisciplinary studies at Langara College in Vancouver, Canada.

Buried Prejudice:
The Bigot in Your Brain

By Siri Carpenter

"There is nothing more painful to me at this stage in my life," Jesse Jackson once told an audience, "than to walk down the street and hear footsteps and start thinking about robbery—then look around and see somebody white and feel relieved."

Jackson's remark illustrates a basic fact of our social existence, one that even a committed black civil-rights leader cannot escape: ideas that we may not endorse—for example, that a black stranger might harm us but a white one probably would not—can nonetheless lodge themselves in our minds and, without our permission or awareness, color our perceptions, expectations and judgments.

Using a variety of sophisticated methods, psychologists have established that people unwittingly hold an astounding assortment of stereotypical beliefs and attitudes about social groups: black and white, female and male, elderly and young, gay and straight, fat and thin. Although these implicit biases inhabit us all, we vary in the particulars, depending on our own group membership, our conscious desire to avoid bias and the contours of our everyday environments. For instance, about two-thirds of whites have an implicit preference for whites over blacks, whereas blacks show no average preference for one race over the other.

Such bias is far more prevalent than the more overt, or explicit, prejudice that we associate with, say, the Ku Klux Klan or the Nazis. That is emphatically *not* to say that explicit prejudice and discrimination have evaporated nor that they are of lesser importance than implicit bias. According to a 2005 federal report, almost 200,000 hate crimes—84 percent of them violent—occur in the U.S. every year.

The persistence of explicit bias in contemporary culture has led some critics to maintain that implicit bias is of secondary concern. But hundreds of studies of implicit bias show that its effects can be equally insidious. Most social psychologists believe that certain scenarios can automatically activate implicit stereotypes and attitudes, which then can affect our perceptions, judgments and behavior. "The data on that are incontrovertible," concludes psychologist Russell H. Fazio of Ohio State University.

Now researchers are probing deeper. They want to know: Where exactly do such biases come from? How much do they influence our outward behavior? And if stereotypes and prejudiced attitudes are burned into our psyches, can learning more about them help to tell each of us how to override them?

Sticking Together

Implicit biases grow out of normal and necessary features of human cognition, such as our tendency to categorize, to form cliques and to absorb social messages and cues. To make sense of the world around us, we put things into groups and remember relations between objects and actions or adjectives: for instance, people automatically note that cars move fast, cookies taste sweet and mosquitoes bite. Without such deductions, we would have a lot more trouble navigating our environment and surviving in it.

Such associations often reside outside conscious understanding; thus, to measure them, psychologists rely on indirect tests that do not depend on people's ability or willingness to reflect on their feelings and thoughts. Several commonly used methods gauge the speed at which people associate words or pictures representing social groups—young and old, female and male, black and white, fat and thin, Democrat and Republican, and so on—with positive or negative words or with particular stereotypic traits.

Because closely associated concepts are essentially linked together in a person's mind, a person will be faster to respond to a related pair of concepts—say, "hammer and nail"—than to an uncoupled pair, such as "hammer and cotton ball." The timing of a person's responses, therefore, can reveal hidden associations such as "black and danger" or "female and frail" that form the basis of implicit prejudice. "One of the questions that people often ask is, 'Can we get rid of implicit associations?'" says psychologist Brian A. Nosek of the University of Virginia. "The answer is no, and we wouldn't want to. If we got rid of them, we would lose a very useful tool that we need for our everyday lives."

The problem arises when we form associations that contradict our intentions, beliefs and values. That is, many people unwittingly associate "female" with "weak," "Arab" with "terrorist," or "black" with "criminal," even though such stereotypes undermine values such as fairness and equality that many of us hold dear.

Self-interest often shores up implicit biases. To bolster our own status, we are predisposed to ascribe superior characteristics to the groups to which we belong, or in-groups, and to exaggerate differences between our own group and outsiders.

Even our basic visual perceptions are skewed toward our in-groups. Many studies have shown that people more readily remember faces of their own race than of other races. In recent years, scientists have begun to probe the neural basis for this phenomenon, known as the same-race memory advantage. In a 2001 study neurosurgeon Alexandra J. Golby, now at Harvard Medical School, and her colleagues used functional magnetic resonance imaging to track people's brain activity while they viewed a series of white and black faces. The researchers found that individuals exhibited greater activity in a brain area involved in face recognition known as the fusiform face area when they viewed faces of their own racial group than when they gazed at faces of a different race. The more strongly a person showed the same-race memory advantage, the greater this brain difference was.

This identification with a group occurs astoundingly quickly. In a 2002 study University of Washington psychologist Anthony G. Greenwald and his colleagues asked 156 people to read the names of four members of two hypothetical teams, Purple and Gold, then spend 45 seconds memorizing the names of the players on just one team. Next, the participants performed two tasks in which they quickly sorted the names of team members. In one task, they grouped members of one team under the concept "win" and those of the other team under "lose," and in the other they linked each team with either "self" or "other." The researchers found that the mere 45 seconds that a person spent thinking about a fictional team made them identify with that team (linking it with "self") and implicitly view its members as "winners."

Some implicit biases appear to be rooted in strong emotions. In a 2004 study Ohio State psychologist Wil A. Cunningham and his colleagues measured white people's brain activity as they viewed a series of white and black faces. The team found that black faces—as compared with white faces—that they flashed for only 30 milliseconds (too quickly for participants to notice them) triggered greater activity in the amygdala, a brain area associated with vigilance and sometimes fear. The effect was most pronounced among people who demonstrated strong implicit racial bias. Provocatively, the same study revealed that when faces were shown for half a second—enough time for participants to consciously process them—black faces instead elicited heightened activity in prefrontal brain areas associated with detecting internal conflicts and controlling responses, hinting that individuals were consciously trying to suppress their implicit associations.

Why might black faces, in particular, provoke vigilance? Northwestern University psychologist Jennifer A. Richeson speculates that American cultural stereotypes linking young black men with crime, violence and danger are so robust that our brains may automatically give preferential attention to blacks as a category, just as they do for threatening animals such as snakes. In a recent unpublished study Richeson and her colleagues found that white college students' visual attention was drawn more quickly to photographs of black versus white men, even though the images were flashed so quickly that participants did not consciously notice them. This heightened vigilance did not appear, however, when the men in the pictures were looking away from the camera. (Averted eye gaze, a signal of submission in humans and other animals, extinguishes explicit perceptions of threat.)

Whatever the neural underpinnings of implicit bias, cultural factors—such as shopworn ethnic jokes, careless catchphrases and playground taunts dispensed by peers, parents or the media—often reinforce such prejudice. Subtle sociocultural signals may carry particularly insidious power. In a recent unpublished study psychologist Luigi Castelli of the University of Padova in Italy and his colleagues examined racial attitudes and behavior in 72 white Italian families. They found that young children's racial preferences were unaffected by their parents' explicit racial attitudes (perhaps because those attitudes were muted). Children whose mothers had more negative implicit attitudes toward blacks, however, tended to choose a white over a black playmate and ascribed more negative traits to a fictional black child than to a white child. Children whose mothers showed less implicit racial bias on an implicit bias test were less likely to exhibit such racial preferences.

Many of our implicit associations about social groups form before we are old enough to consider them rationally. In an unpublished experiment Mahzarin R. Banaji, a psychologist at Harvard University, and Yarrow Dunham, now a psychologist at the University of California, Merced, found that white preschoolers tended to categorize racially ambiguous angry faces as black rather than white; they did not do so for happy faces. And a 2006 study by Banaji and Harvard graduate student Andrew S. Baron shows that full-fledged implicit racial bias emerges by age six—and never retreats. "These filters through which people see the world are present very early," Baron concludes.

Dangerous Games

On February 4, 1999, four New York City police officers knocked on the apartment door of a 23-year-old West African immigrant named Amadou Diallo. They intended to question him because his physical description matched that of a suspected rapist. Moments later Diallo lay dead. The officers, believing that Diallo was reaching for a gun, had fired 41 shots at him, 19 of which struck their target. The item that Diallo had been pulling from his pocket was not a gun but his wallet. The officers were charged with second-degree murder but argued that at the time of the shooting they believed their lives were in danger. Their argument was successful, and they were acquitted.

In the Diallo case, the officers' split-second decision to open fire had massive, and tragic, consequences, and the court proceedings and public outcry that followed the shooting raised a number of troubling questions. To what degree are our decisions swayed by implicit social biases? How do those implicit biases interact with our more deliberate choices?

A growing body of work indicates that implicit attitudes do, in fact, contaminate our behavior. Reflexive actions and snap judgments may be especially vulnerable to implicit associations. A number of studies have shown, for instance, that both blacks and whites tend to mistake a harmless object such as a cell phone or hand tool for a gun if a black face accompanies the object. This "weapon bias" is especially strong when people have to judge the situation very quickly.

In a 2002 study of racial attitudes and nonverbal behavior, psychologist John F. Dovidio, now at Yale University, and his colleagues measured explicit and implicit racial attitudes among 40 white college students. The researchers then asked the white participants to chat with one black and one white person while the researchers videotaped the interaction. Dovidio and his colleagues found that in these interracial interactions, the white participants' explicit attitudes best predicted the kinds of behavior they could easily control, such as the friendliness of their spoken words. Participants' nonverbal signals, however, such as the amount of eye contact they made, depended on their implicit attitudes.

As a result, Dovidio says, whites and blacks came away from the conversation with very different impressions of how it had gone. Whites typically thought the interactions had gone well, but blacks, attuned to whites' nonverbal behavior, thought otherwise. Blacks also assumed that the whites were conscious of their nonverbal behavior and blamed white prejudice. "Our society is really characterized by this lack of perspective," Dovidio says. "Understanding both implicit and explicit attitudes helps you understand how whites and blacks could look at the same thing and not understand how the other person saw it differently."

Implicit biases can infect more deliberate decisions, too. In a 2007 study Rutgers University psychologists Laurie A. Rudman and Richard D. Ashmore found that white people who exhibited greater implicit bias toward black people also reported a stronger tendency to engage in a variety of discriminatory acts in their everyday lives. These included avoiding or excluding blacks socially, uttering racial slurs and jokes, and insulting, threatening or physically harming black people.

In a second study reported in the same paper, Rudman and Ashmore set up a laboratory scenario to further examine the link between implicit bias against Jews, Asians and blacks and discriminatory behavior toward each of those groups. They asked research participants to examine a budget proposal ostensibly under consideration at their university and to make recommendations for allocating funding to student organizations. Students who exhibited greater implicit bias toward a given minority group tended to suggest budgets that discriminated more against organizations devoted to that group's interests.

Implicit bias may sway hiring decisions. In a recent unpublished field experiment economist Dan-Olof Rooth of the University of Kalmar in Sweden sent corporate employers identical job applications on behalf of fictional male candidates—under either Arab-Muslim or Swedish names. Next he tracked down the 193 human resources professionals who had evaluated the applications and measured their implicit biases concerning Arab-Muslim men. Rooth discovered that the greater the employer's bias, the less likely he or she was to call an applicant with a name such as Mohammed or Reza for an interview. Employers' explicit attitudes toward Muslims did not correspond to their decision to interview (or fail to consider) someone with a Muslim name, possibly because many recruiters were reluctant to reveal those attitudes.

Unconscious racial bias may also infect critical medical decisions. In a 2007 study Banaji and her Harvard colleagues presented 287 internal medicine and emergency care physicians with a photograph and brief clinical vignette describing a middle-aged patient—in some cases black and in others white—who came to the hospital complaining of chest pain. Most physicians did not acknowledge racial bias, but on average they showed (on an implicit bias test) a moderate to large implicit antiblack bias. And the greater a physician's racial bias, the less likely he or she was to give a black patient clot-busting thrombolytic drugs.

Beating Back Prejudice

Researchers long believed that because implicit associations develop early in our lives, and because we are often unaware of their influence, they may be virtually impervious to change. But recent work suggests that we can reshape our implicit attitudes and beliefs—or at least curb their effects on our behavior.

Seeing targeted groups in more favorable social contexts can help thwart biased attitudes. In laboratory studies, seeing a black face with a church as a background, instead of a dilapidated street corner, considering familiar examples of admired blacks such as actor Denzel Washington and athlete Michael Jordan, and reading about Arab-Muslims' positive contributions to society all weaken people's implicit racial and ethnic biases. In real college classrooms, students taking a course on prejudice reduction who had a black professor showed greater reductions in both implicit and explicit prejudice at the end of the semester than did those who had a white professor. And in a recent unpublished study Nilanjana Dasgupta, a psychologist at the University of Massachusetts Amherst, found that female engineering students who had a male professor held negative implicit attitudes toward math and implicitly viewed math as masculine. Students with a female engineering professor did not.

More than half a century ago the eminent social psychologist Gordon Allport called group labels "nouns that cut slices," pointing to the power of mere words to shape how we categorize and perceive others. New research underscores that words exert equal potency at an implicit level. In a 2003 study Harvard psychologist Jason Mitchell, along with Nosek and Banaji, instructed white female college students to sort a series of stereotypically black female and white male names according to either race or gender. The group found that categorizing the names according to their race prompted a prowhite bias, but categorizing the same set of names according to their gender prompted an implicit profemale (and hence problack) bias. "These attitudes can form quickly, and they can change quickly" if we restructure our environments to crowd out stereotypical associations and replace them with egalitarian ones, Dasgupta concludes.

In other words, changes in external stimuli, many of which lie outside our control, can trick our brains into making new associations. But an even more obvious tactic would be to confront such biases head-on with conscious effort. And some evidence suggests willpower can work. Among the doctors in the thrombolytic drug study who were aware of the study's purpose, those who showed more implicit racial bias were more likely to prescribe thrombolytic treatment to black patients than were those with less bias, suggesting that recognizing the presence of implicit bias helped them offset it.

In addition, people who report a strong personal motivation to be nonprejudiced tend to harbor less implicit bias. And some studies indicate that people who are good at using logic and willpower to control their more primitive urges, such as trained meditators, exhibit less implicit bias. Brain research suggests that the people who are best at inhibiting implicit stereotypes are those who are especially skilled at detecting mismatches between their intentions and their actions.

But wresting control over automatic processes is tiring and can backfire. If people leave interracial interactions feeling mentally and emotionally drained, they may simply avoid contact with people of a different race or foreign culture. "If you boil it down, the solution sounds kind of easy: just maximize control," says psychologist

B. Keith Payne of the University of North Carolina at Chapel Hill. "But how do you do that? As it plays out in the real world, it's not so easy."

Other research suggests that developing simple but concrete plans to supplant stereotypes in particular situations can also short-circuit implicit biases. In an unpublished study Payne and his colleague Brandon D. Stewart, now a postdoctoral fellow at the University of Queensland in Australia, found that those who simply resolved to think of the word "safe" whenever they saw a black face showed dramatic reductions in implicit racial bias. "You don't necessarily have to beat people over the head with it," Payne observes. "You can just have this little plan in your pocket [think 'safe'] that you can pull out when you need it. Once you've gone to the work of making that specific plan, it becomes automatic."

Taking Control

Despite such data, some psychologists still question the concept of implicit bias. In a 2004 article in the journal *Psychological Inquiry*, psychologists Hal R. Arkes of Ohio State and Philip E. Tetlock of the University of California, Berkeley, suggest that implicit associations between, for example, black people and negative words may not necessarily reflect implicit hostility toward blacks. They could as easily reflect other negative feelings, such as shame about black people's historical treatment at the hands of whites. They also argue that any unfavorable associations about black people we do hold may simply echo shared knowledge of stereotypes in the culture. In that sense, Arkes and Tetlock maintain, implicit measures do not signify anything meaningful about people's internal state, nor do they deserve to be labeled "prejudiced"—a term they feel should be reserved for attitudes a person deliberately endorses.

Others dispute the significance of such a distinction. "There is no clear boundary between the self and society—and this may be particularly true at the automatic level," write Rudman and Ashmore in a 2007 article in the journal *Group Processes & Intergroup*

Relations. "Growing up in a culture where some people are valued more than others is likely to permeate our private orientations, no matter how discomfiting the fact."

If we accept this tenet of the human condition, then we have a choice about how to respond. We can respond with sadness or, worse, with apathy. Or we can react with a determination to overcome bias. "The capacity for change is deep and great in us," Banaji says. "But do we want the change? That's the question for each of us as individuals—individual scientists, and teachers, and judges, and businesspeople, and the communities to which we belong."

About the Author

Siri Carpenter is a social psychologist and freelance science writer specializing in behavioral science topics. In the 1990s, she studied implicit gender bias under Mahzarin R. Banaji, then at Yale University. She is also co-author of the book Visualizing Psychology *(John Wiley & Sons, 2007). She lives in Madison, Wisconsin.*

How to Think About Implicit Bias

By Keith Payne, Laura Niemi and John M. Doris

When's the last time a stereotype popped into your mind? If you are like most people, the authors included, it happens all the time. That doesn't make you a racist, sexist or whateverist. It just means your brain is working properly, noticing patterns and making generalizations. But the same thought processes that make people smart can also make them biased. This tendency for stereotype-confirming thoughts to pass spontaneously through our minds is what psychologists call implicit bias. It sets people up to overgeneralize, sometimes leading to discrimination even when people feel they are being fair.

Studies of implicit bias have recently drawn ire from both the right and the left. For the right, talk of implicit bias is just another instance of progressives seeing injustice under every bush. For the left, implicit bias diverts attention from more damaging instances of explicit bigotry. Debates have become heated and have leaped from scientific journals to the popular press. Along the way, some important points have been lost. We highlight two misunderstandings that anyone who wants to understand implicit bias should know about.

First, much of the controversy centers on the most famous implicit bias test, the Implicit Association Test (IAT). A majority of people taking this test show evidence of implicit bias, suggesting that most individuals are implicitly biased even if they do not think of themselves as prejudiced. As with any measure, the test does have limitations. The stability of the test is low, meaning that if you take the same test a few weeks apart, you might score very differently. And the correlation between a person's IAT scores and discriminatory behavior is often small.

The IAT is a measure, and it doesn't follow from a particular measure being flawed that the *phenomenon* we are attempting to measure is not real. Drawing that conclusion is to commit the Divining Rod Fallacy: just because a rod doesn't find water doesn't mean there's no such thing as water. A smarter move is to ask, "What does the other evidence show?"

In fact, there is lots of other evidence. There are perceptual illusions, for example, in which white subjects perceive Black faces as angrier than white faces with the same expression. Race can bias people to see harmless objects as weapons when they are in the hands of Black men and to dislike abstract images that are paired with Black faces. And there are dozens of variants of laboratory tasks finding that most participants are faster to identify bad words paired with Black faces than white faces. None of these measures is without limitations, but they show the same pattern of reliable bias as the IAT. There is a mountain of evidence—independent of any single test—that implicit bias is real.

The second misunderstanding is about what scientists mean when they say a measure predicts behavior. One frequent complaint is that an individual's IAT score doesn't tell you whether the person will discriminate on a particular occasion. This is to commit the Palm Reading Fallacy: unlike palm readers, research psychologists aren't usually in the business of telling you, as an individual, what your life holds in store. Most measures in psychology, from aptitude tests to personality scales, are useful for predicting how *groups* will respond *on average*, not forecasting how particular *individuals* will behave.

The difference is crucial. Knowing that an employee scored high on conscientiousness won't tell you much about whether her work will be careful or sloppy if you inspect it right now. But if a large company hires hundreds of employees who are all conscientious, this will likely pay off with a small but consistent increase in careful work on average.

Implicit bias researchers have always warned against using the tests for predicting individual outcomes, such as how a particular manager will behave in job interviews—they've never been in the palm-reading business. What the IAT does, and does well, is predict average outcomes across larger entities such as counties, cities or states. For example, metro areas with greater average implicit bias have larger racial disparities in police shootings. And counties with greater average implicit bias have larger racial disparities in infant health problems. These correlations are important: the lives of Black citizens and newborn Black babies depend on them.

Field experiments demonstrate that real-world discrimination continues and is widespread. White applicants get about 50 percent more callbacks than Black applicants with the same resumes; college professors are 26 percent more likely to respond to a student's e-mail when it is signed by Brad rather than Lamar; and physicians recommend less pain medication for Black patients than white patients with the same injury.

Today managers are unlikely to announce that white job applicants should be chosen over Black applicants, and physicians don't declare that Black people feel less pain than whites. Yet the widespread pattern of discrimination and disparities seen in field studies persists. It bears a much closer resemblance to the widespread stereotypical thoughts seen on implicit bias tests than to the survey studies in which most people present themselves as unbiased.

One reason people on both the right and the left are skeptical of implicit bias might be pretty simple: it isn't nice to think we aren't very nice. It would be comforting to conclude, when we don't consciously entertain impure intentions, that all of our intentions are pure. Unfortunately, we can't conclude that: many of us are more biased than we realize. And that is an important cause of injustice—whether you know it or not.

About the Authors

Keith Payne is a professor in psychology and neuroscience at the University of North Carolina at Chapel Hill. He is the author of The Broken Ladder: How Inequality Affects the Way We Think, Live, and Die *(Viking, 2017).*

Laura Niemi is an assistant professor in the Department of Psychology at Cornell University. She researches moral judgment and the implications of differences in moral values.

John M. Doris is the Peter L. Dyson Professor of Ethics in Organizations and Life at the Charles H. Dyson School of Applied Economics and Management and a professor at the Sage School of Philosophy at Cornell University.

The Flexibility of Racial Bias

By Mina Cikara and Jay Van Bavel

In 2013 the Black Lives Matter movement began after George Zimmerman was acquitted for shooting Trayvon Martin, a 17-year-old Black teen. The following year the movement triggered national protests after the killing of Michael Brown and Eric Garner. In 2020 the murders of Breonna Taylor and George Floyd led to global protests against racial injustice. These are not isolated incidents. Institutional and systemic racism reinforce discrimination in countless situations, including hiring, sentencing, housing and mortgage lending.

It would be easy to see in all this powerful evidence that racism is a permanent fixture in America's social fabric and even, perhaps, an inevitable aspect of human nature. Indeed, the mere act of labeling others according to their age, gender or race is a reflexive habit of the human mind. Social groupings such as race that we have come to think of as "categories" influence our thinking quickly, often outside of our awareness. Extensive research has found that these implicit racial biases—subconscious negative thoughts and feelings about people from other races—are automatic, pervasive and difficult to suppress. Neuroscientists have explored racial prejudice by exposing people to images of faces while scanning their brains in functional MRI machines. Early studies found that when people viewed faces of another race, the amount of activity in the amygdala—a small brain structure associated with experiencing emotions, including fear—was associated with individual differences on measures of implicit racial bias.

This work has led many to conclude that racial biases might be part of a primitive—and possibly hardwired—neural fear response to racial out-groups. These results, coupled with pervasive discrimination and ongoing violence, paint a bleak picture. But scientists have learned that the amygdala's role in implicit bias is more complex than it first seemed. Moreover, recent findings from psychology and neuroscience have found that individual prejudices and their neural underpinnings are surprisingly flexible. It seems that the key factor in predicting our responses to other groups is not simply their race but rather whether we believe "they" are with us or against us. Group allegiances can turn on a dime, in some cases effectively "erasing race" from people's judgments or creating new classes of enemies (for example, the increase in anti-Muslim hate crimes after 9/11). This new evidence of the flexibility of implicit bias illustrates that we are not hardwired to be racist—and, furthermore, that prejudice can be reduced under the right conditions.

There is little question that categories such as race, gender, age, and other social categories play a major role in shaping the biases and stereotypes that people bring to bear in their judgments of others. But research has found that how people categorize themselves may be just as fundamental to understanding prejudice as how they categorize others. When people categorize themselves as part of a group, their self-concept shifts from the individual ("I") to the collective level ("us"). People form groups rapidly and favor members of their own group even when groups are formed on arbitrary grounds, such as the simple flip of a coin. These findings highlight the remarkable ease with which humans form *coalitions*. And this seems to be a universal human tendency—every culture ever studied displays this same propensity.

Many studies have shown that coalition-based preferences override race-based preferences. For instance, our research has revealed that the simple act of placing people on a mixed-race team can diminish their automatic racial bias. In a series of experiments, white participants who were randomly placed on a mixed-race team—the Tigers or Lions—showed little evidence of implicit racial bias. Merely belonging to a mixed-race team triggered positive automatic associations with all the members of their own group, regardless of race. Being part of one of these seemingly trivial mixed-race groups produced similar effects on brain activity—the amygdala responded to team membership rather than race.

The same dynamic is at play in politics. For example, both Democrats and Republicans in the U.S. favor the resumes of those affiliated with their political party much more than they favor those who share their race. These coalition-based preferences remain powerful even in the absence of the animosity present in electoral politics. Taken together, these studies indicate that momentary changes in group membership can override the influence of race on the way we see, think about and feel toward people who are different from ourselves.

Although these coalition-based distinctions might be the most basic building block of bias, they say little about the other factors that cause group conflict. Why do some groups get ignored while others get attacked? Whenever we encounter a new person or group, we are motivated to answer two questions as quickly as possible: Is this person a friend or foe, and are they capable of enacting their intentions toward me? In other words, once we have determined that someone is a member of an out-group, we need to determine what kind. The nature of the relations between groups—Are they cooperative or competitive, or neither?—and their relative status—Do they have access to resources?—largely determine the course of intergroup interactions.

Groups that are seen as competitive with one's interests, and capable of enacting their opposing intentions, are much more likely to be targets of hostility than more benevolent (elderly) or powerless (homeless) groups. This is one reason why sports rivalries have such psychological potency. For instance, fans of the Boston Red Sox are more likely to feel pleasure, and exhibit reward-related neural responses, at the misfortunes of the archrival New York Yankees than other baseball teams (and vice versa)—especially in the midst of a tight playoff race. (How much fans take pleasure in the misfortunes of their rivals is also linked to how likely they would be to harm fans from the other team.)

Just as a particular person's group membership can be flexible, so, too, are the relations between groups. Groups that have previously had cordial relations may become rivals (and vice versa). Indeed, psychological and biological responses to out-group members can change, depending on whether or not that out-group is perceived as threatening. For example, people exhibit greater pleasure—they smile—in response to the misfortunes of stereotypically competitive groups (investment bankers); however, this malicious pleasure is reduced when you provide participants with counterstereotypic information (investment bankers who are working with small companies to help them weather an economic downturn). Competition between "us" and "them" can even distort our judgments of distance, making threatening out-groups seem much closer than they really are. These distorted perceptions can serve to amplify intergroup discrimination: the more different and distant "they" are, the easier it is to disrespect and harm them.

Thus, not all out-groups are treated the same: some elicit indifference, whereas others become targets of antipathy. Stereotypically threatening groups are especially likely to be targeted with violence, but those stereotypes can be tempered with other information. If perceptions of intergroup relations can be changed, individuals may overcome hostility toward perceived foes and become more responsive to one another's grievances.

The flexible nature of both group membership and intergroup relations offers reason to be cautiously optimistic about the potential for greater cooperation among groups in conflict (be they Black versus white or citizens versus police). One strategy is to bring multiple groups together around a common goal. For example, in an experiment conducted during the fiercely contested 2008 Democratic presidential primary process, Hillary Clinton and Barack Obama supporters gave more money to strangers who supported the same primary candidate (compared with the rival candidate). Two months later, after the Democratic National Convention, the supporters of both candidates coalesced around the party nominee—Barack Obama—and this bias disappeared.

We have found that creating a sense of cohesion between competitive groups can increase empathy for the suffering of our rivals. These strategies can help reduce aggression toward out-groups, which is critical for creating more chances for constructive dialogue addressing greater social injustices.

Of course, instilling a sense of common identity and cooperation is extremely difficult in entrenched intergroup conflicts, but when it happens, the benefits are obvious. Consider how the community leaders in New York City and in Ferguson, Mo., responded differently to protests against police brutality—in N.Y.C., political leaders expressed grief and concern over police brutality and moved quickly to make policy changes in policing, whereas the leaders and police in Ferguson suppressed protests with high-tech military vehicles and riot gear. In the first case, groups came together with a common goal—to increase the safety of everyone in the community; in the latter, the actions of the police likely reinforced the "us" and "them" distinctions and amplified discord.

Tragically, these types of conflicts continue to roil the country. And the fact that our modern stereotypes and prejudices are tightly linked to historical mistreatment and oppression makes it very hard to find sustainable solutions to these problems. Understanding the psychology and neuroscience of social identity and intergroup relations cannot undo the effects of systemic racism and discriminatory practices; however, it can offer insights into the psychological processes responsible for escalating—or de-escalating—the tension between, for example, civilians and police officers.

Even in cases where it isn't possible to create a common identity among groups in conflict, it may be possible to blur the boundaries between groups. In one recent experiment, we sorted participants into groups—red versus blue—competing for a cash prize. Half of the participants were randomly assigned to see a picture of a segregated social network of all the players, in which red dots clustered together, blue dots clustered together, and the two clusters were separated by white space. The other half of the participants saw an integrated social network in which the red and blue dots were mixed together in one large cluster. Participants who thought the two teams were interconnected with one another reported greater empathy for the out-group players compared with those who had seen the segregated network. Thus, reminding people that individuals could be connected to one another despite being from different groups may be another way to build trust and understanding among them.

A mere month before Freddie Gray died in Baltimore in police custody, President Obama addressed the nation on the 50th anniversary of Bloody Sunday in Selma: "We do a disservice to the cause of justice by intimating that bias and discrimination are immutable or that racial division is inherent to America. To deny ... progress—our progress—would be to rob us of our own agency; our responsibility to do what we can to make America better."

Research from psychology and neuroscience indicates that we, as individuals, possess this capacity. Understanding this fact means that we have a responsibility to reduce prejudice and discrimination. Of course, reducing prejudice is not sufficient to usher in racial equality or peace. Even when the level of prejudice against particular out-groups decreases, it does not imply that the level of institutional discrimination against these or other groups will necessarily improve. In many cases, even egalitarian people can perpetuate harm if the systems in place are already unjust.

Ultimately only collective action and institutional evolution can address systemic racism. The science, however, is clear on one thing: individual bias and discrimination are changeable. Race-based prejudice and discrimination, in particular, are created and reinforced by many social factors, but they are not inevitable consequences of our biology. We hope that understanding how coalitional thinking impacts intergroup relations will make it easier for us to affect real social change going forward.

About the Authors

Mina Cikara is an assistant professor of psychology and director of the Intergroup Neuroscience Lab at Harvard University. Her research examines the conditions under which groups and individuals are denied social value, agency and empathy.

Jay Van Bavel is an assistant professor of psychology and director of the Social Identity and Morality Laboratory at New York University. He studies how our collective concerns—group identities, moral values and political beliefs—alter our perceptions and evaluations of the world around us.

Microaggressions: Death by a Thousand Cuts

By Derald Wing Sue

My research and work on racial microaggressions began through a series of lifelong experiences and observations of interpersonal racial encounters. For example, I am a second-generation Asian-American, born and raised in the U.S. Yet despite that fact, I receive constant compliments for speaking "good" English. On crowded New York City subway trains, with all seats taken, I noticed that there would always be an empty one next to a Black passenger. These examples and countless incidents are what we call "racial microaggressions."

Microaggressions are the everyday slights, insults, put-downs, invalidations and offensive behaviors that people of marginalized groups experience in daily interactions with generally well-intentioned people who may be unaware of their impact. Microaggressions are reflections of implicit bias or prejudicial beliefs and attitudes beyond the level of conscious awareness. Social psychologists have studied implicit bias for decades, along with the role it plays in human behavior. Almost any marginalized group can be the object of microaggressions. There are racial, gender, LGBTQ and disability microaggressions that occur daily to these groups.

Most individuals who commit microaggressions view themselves as moral and decent human beings who never would consciously discriminate against another person. Yet it is important to acknowledge that none of us is immune from inheriting the racial, gender or sexual orientation biases of our society. Let us return to the two opening examples to understand more fully the manifestation, dynamics and impact of microaggressions.

Microaggressions often contain a "metacommunication" or hidden message to the target, which reveals a biased belief or attitude. Although the perpetrator believes that he or she is praising me for speaking good English, the underlying message to me is, "You are a perpetual foreigner in your own country. You are not a true American, because true Americans are light-skinned."

The reluctance to sit next to Black people on the subway is a message that "you are to be avoided because you are potentially dangerous, a criminal or up to no good." Many of my Black friends tell tales of how they enter an elevator with a single white female and how she tenses up, clutches her purse more tightly and moves away in fear.

Microaggressions often convey to targets the message that they are foreigners, criminals, dangerous, a threat or subhuman. Our research labels these messages as themes: for Asian-Americans and Latinx-Americans, that you are a perpetual alien in your own country; for Black people, that you might be a criminal; for people who identify as LGBTQ, that you're a sinner; and, if you're a woman, that you can be sexually objectified.

The saying that "sticks and stones may break my bones, but words will never hurt me" expresses a belief that microaggressions are harmless, small, trivial and insignificant. Critics of microaggression theory believe that we are "making a mountain out of a molehill" and that such incidents are no different from the everyday incivilities that a white person might experience from a rude clerk. Our research, however, reveals major differences that account for their greater harmful and detrimental impact on people of color:

- Microaggressions are constant and continual in the life experience of people of color. They experience these offensive behaviors every day from the moment they awaken in the morning until they go to sleep at night and from the time they are born until they die.
- Microaggressions are cumulative, and any one offense or put-down may represent the straw that breaks the camel's back.
- Microaggressions are constant reminders to people of color that they are second-class citizens.
- Microaggressions are energy-depleting and lead to the concept of "racial battle fatigue."

- Microaggressions symbolize past historic injustices, such as the enslavement of Africans, the taking away of land from the Indigenous people of this country, and the incarceration of Japanese-Americans during World War II.

These distinctions have led psychologists to refer to everyday slights or indignities experienced by people of color as "death by a thousand cuts." Far from being harmless and benign, microaggressions have a macro impact on targets. A whole body of research supports this conclusion. They increase stress in the lives of people of color, lower emotional well-being, increase depression and negative feelings, assail the mental health of recipients, impede learning and problem-solving, impair employee performance and take a heavy toll on the physical well-being of targets. Equally important are findings that microaggressions lower the standard of living of groups of color and create inequities in employment, education and health care.

In closing, I share with you the words of Martin Luther King, Jr., from his "Letter from Birmingham Jail": "We will have to repent in this generation not merely for the hateful words and actions of the bad people but for the appalling silence of the good people." These words have led us to ask an important question: What can well-meaning allies and bystanders do to disarm and dismantle microaggressions they observe?

Our research team at Teachers College, Columbia University, has begun to study and develop antibias education and training strategies called microinterventions. These are the everyday antibias actions that can be taken by targets, parents, significant others, allies and well-intentioned bystanders to counteract, challenge, diminish or neutralize individual and systemic expressions of prejudice, bigotry and discrimination.

We have been able to organize microinterventions into four strategic goals: (1) make the "invisible" visible, (2) educate the perpetrator, (3) disarm the microaggression, and (4) seek outside support and help. For those interested in our latest research venture, much of the information can be found in our

2020 *American Psychologist* article entitled "Disarming Racial Microaggressions: Microintervention Strategies for Targets, White Allies, and Bystanders."

As Dr. King says, silence and inaction in the face of moral transgressions are complicity and collusion. As a society, each of us has a moral responsibility to take action against bias and bigotry.

About the Author

Derald Wing Sue is a professor of psychology and education at Teachers College, Columbia University. He is the author of Microaggressions in Everyday Life *(John Wiley, 2020) and* Microintervention Strategies: What You Can Do to Disarm and Dismantle Individual and Systemic Racism and Bias *(John Wiley, 2020).*

Section 2: Racism in Health and Psychology

2.1 Inequality Before Birth Contributes to Health Inequality in Adults
 By Janet Currie

2.2 How Doctors Can Confront Racial Bias in Medicine
 By Rachel Pearson

2.3 To Achieve Mental Health Equity, Dismantle Social Injustice
 By Ruth S. Shim and Sarah Y. Vinson

2.4 Why Racism, Not Race, Is a Risk Factor for Dying of COVID-19
 By Claudia Wallis

2.5 Teaching Antiracism to the Next Generation of Doctors
 By Rupinder Kaur Legha

Inequality Before Birth Contributes to Health Inequality in Adults

By Janet Currie

The COVID-19 pandemic has disproportionately hurt members of minority communities in the U.S. As of July 2020, 73.7 Black people out of every 100,000 had died of the coronavirus—compared with 32.4 of every 100,000 white people. Structural racism accounts for much of this disparity. Black people are more likely to have jobs that require them to leave their homes and to commute by public transport, for example, both of which increase the chances of getting infected. They are also more likely to get grievously ill when the virus strikes. As of June 2020, the hospitalization rate for those who tested positive for SARS-CoV-2 infection was more than four times higher for Black people than for non-Hispanic white people.

One reason for this alarming ratio is that Black people have higher rates of diabetes, hypertension and asthma—ailments linked to worse outcomes after infection with the coronavirus. Decades of research show that these health conditions, usually diagnosed in adulthood, can reflect hardships experienced while in the womb. Children do not start on a level playing field at birth. Risk factors linked to maternal poverty—such as malnutrition, smoking, exposure to pollution, stress or lack of health care during pregnancy—can predispose babies to future disease. And mothers from minority communities were and are more likely to be subjected to these risks.

Today's older Black Americans—those most endangered by COVID-19—are more likely than not to have been born into poverty. In 1959, 55 percent of Black people in the U.S. had incomes below the poverty level, compared with fewer than 10 percent of white people. Nowadays 20 percent of Black Americans live below the poverty line, whereas the poverty rate for white Americans remains roughly the same. Despite the reduction in income inequality between these groups, ongoing racism works through circuitous routes to worsen the odds for minority infants. For example, partly because of a history of redlining (practices through which financial and other institutions made it difficult for Black families to buy homes in predominantly white areas), even better-off Black people are more likely to live in polluted areas than are poorer white people—with a corresponding impact on fetal health. Worryingly, people disadvantaged in utero are more likely to have lower earnings and educational attainments, so that the effects of poverty and discrimination can span generations.

Researchers now have hard evidence that targeted programs can improve health and reduce inequality. Expansions of public health insurance offered to women, infants and children under Medicaid and the Children's Health Insurance Program have already had a tremendous effect, improving the health and well-being of a generation—with the largest impacts on Black children. And interventions after birth can often reverse much of the damage suffered prenatally. Along with other researchers, I have shown that nutrition programs for pregnant women, infants and children; home visits by nurses during pregnancy and after childbirth; high-quality child care; and income support can improve the outcomes for disadvantaged children. Such interventions came too late to help those born in the 1950s or earlier, but they have narrowed the health gaps between poor and rich children, as well as between white and Black children, in the subsequent decades.

Enormous disparities in health and vulnerability remain, however, and raise disturbing questions about how children born to poorer mothers during the current pandemic, with all its social and economic dislocations, will fare. Alarmingly, just before the pandemic hit, many of the most essential programs were being cut back. Since the beginning of 2018, more than a million children have lost Medicaid coverage because of new work requirements and other regulations, and many have become uninsured. Now that the COVID death toll has exposed stark inequalities in health status and their attendant risks, Americans must act urgently to reverse these setbacks and to strengthen public health systems and the social safety net, with special attention to the care of mothers, infants and children.

The Hunger Winter

Decades of careful observation and analysis have gone into uncovering the manifold ways in which the fetal environment affects the future health and prospects of a child, and much remains mysterious. It would be unethical to run experiments to measure the toll on a fetus of, say, malnutrition or pollution. But we can look for so-called natural experiments—the (sometimes horrific) events that cause variations in these factors in ways that mimic an actual experiment. The late epidemiologist David Barker argued in the 1980s that poor nutrition during pregnancy could "program" babies in the womb to develop future ailments such as obesity, heart disease and diabetes. Initial evidence for such ideas came from studies of the Dutch "Hunger Winter." In October 1944 Nazi occupiers cut off food supplies to the Netherlands, and by April 1945 mass starvation had set in. Decades later military, medical and employment records showed that adult men whose mothers were exposed to the famine while pregnant with them were twice as likely to be obese as other men and were more likely to have schizophrenia, diabetes or heart disease.

Anyone born in the Netherlands during the famine is part of a cohort that can be followed over time through a variety of records. Nowadays many researchers, including me, look for natural experiments to delineate such cohorts and thereby tease out the long-term impacts of various harms experienced in utero. We also rely heavily on the most widely available measure of newborn health: birth weight. A baby may have "low" birth weight, defined as less than 2,500 grams (about 5.5 pounds), or "very low" birth weight of less than 1,500 grams (3.3 pounds). The lower the birth weight, the higher the risk of infant death. We have made enormous progress in saving premature babies, but low-birth-weight children are still at much higher risk for complications such as brain bleeds and respiratory problems that can lead to long-term disability.

In recent years computer analysis of large-scale electronic records has made it possible to connect infant health, as measured by birth weight, to long-term outcomes not just for cohorts but also for individuals. Studies of twins or siblings, who have similar genetic and social inheritance, show that those with lower birth weight are more likely to have asthma or attention deficit hyperactivity disorder (ADHD) when they get older. Several studies also show that lower-birth-weight twins or siblings have worse scores on standardized tests. As adults, they are more likely to have lower wages, to reside in lower-income areas or to be on disability-assistance programs. In combination, cohort and sibling studies demonstrate that low birth weight is predictive of several adverse health outcomes later in life, including increased probabilities of asthma, heart disease, diabetes, obesity and some mental health conditions.

Birth weight does not capture all aspects of a child's health: a fetus gains most of its weight in the third trimester, for example, but many studies find that shocks in the first trimester are particularly harmful. I nonetheless use the measure in my studies because it is important and commonly available, having been recorded for tens of millions of babies for decades.

Significantly, low birth weight is much more common among infants born to poor and minority mothers. In 2016 13.5 percent of Black mothers had low-birth-weight babies, compared with 7.0 percent of non-Hispanic whites and 7.3 percent of Hispanic mothers. Among those with college educations, 9.6 percent of Black mothers had low-birth-weight babies, compared with 3.7 percent of non-Hispanic white mothers. These inequalities in health at birth reflect large differences in exposure to several factors that affect fetal health.

The Poverty Connection

As already noted, the quality of a mother's nutrition substantially influences the health of her babies. In 1962 geneticist James V.

Neel hypothesized that a so-called thrifty gene had programmed humankind's hunter-gatherer ancestors to hold on to every calorie they could get and that in modern times, that tendency, combined with an abundance of high-calorie foods, led to obesity and diabetes. Recent studies on laboratory animals indicate, however, that the link between starvation and disease is not genetic in origin but epigenetic, altering how certain genes are "expressed" as proteins. Prolonged calorie deprivation in a pregnant mouse, for example, prompts changes in gene expression in her offspring that predispose them to diabetes. What is more, the effect may be transmitted through generations.

Outright starvation is now rare in developed countries, but poorer mothers in the U.S. often lack a diet rich in fruits and vegetables, which contain essential micronutrients. Deficiencies in folate intake during pregnancy are linked to neural tube defects in children, for example.

At present, one of the leading causes of low birth weight in the U.S. is smoking during pregnancy. In the 1950s pregnant women were told that smoking was safe for their babies. Roughly half of all new mothers in 1960 reported smoking while pregnant. Today, thanks to public education campaigns, indoor-smoking bans and higher cigarette taxes, only 7.2 percent of pregnant women say that they smoke. And 55 percent of women who smoked in the three months before they got pregnant quit for at least the duration of their pregnancy.

Possibly because going to college places women in a milieu where smoking is strongly discouraged, mothers with higher education levels are less likely to smoke. Among mothers with less than a high school education, 11.7 percent smoke, compared with 1 percent of mothers with a bachelor's degree.

Among the many harmful chemicals in cigarette smoke is carbon monoxide (CO), which restricts the amount of oxygen carried by the blood to the fetus. In addition, nicotine affects the development of blood vessels in the uterus and disrupts developing neurotransmitter systems, leading to poorer psychological outcomes. Maternal cigarette smoking during pregnancy has also been associated with epigenetic changes in the fetus, although how these alterations affect an individual in later years remains mysterious. The recent surge in vaping, which delivers high doses of nicotine and which surveys show has been tried by almost 40 percent of high school seniors, is an extremely worrying development that could have long-term implications for fetal and infant health.

Yet another significant source of harm for fetuses is pollution. Pregnant women may be exposed to thousands of toxic chemicals in the air, water, soil and sundry products at home and at work. Complicating matters, each pollutant acts in a different way. Particulates in the atmosphere are thought to cause inflammation throughout the body, which has been linked to preterm labor and, consequently, to low birth weight. Lead, ingested through water or air, crosses the placenta to accumulate in the fetus and harm brain development. In 2005 Jessica Wolpaw Reyes of Amherst College showed that the phaseout of leaded gasoline in the U.S. led to a decrease of up to 4 percent in infant mortality and low birth weight.

A fetus may also receive less oxygen if its mother inhales CO from vehicle exhaust. In a 2009 study of mothers who lived near pollution monitors, my co-workers and I found that high levels of ambient CO were correlated with reduced birth weight. Worryingly, the effects of CO from air pollution are five times greater for smokers than for nonsmokers.

Reducing pollution can have immediate benefits for pregnant women and newborns. In a 2011 study of babies born in New Jersey and Pennsylvania, Reed Walker of the University of California, Berkeley, and I focused on mothers who lived near E-ZPass electronic toll plazas before and after they began operating. We compared them with mothers who lived a little farther from the toll plazas but along the same busy roads. Both groups of mothers were exposed to traffic, but before E-ZPass, the mothers near the toll plazas were exposed to more pollution because cars idled while waiting to pay the tolls. E-ZPass greatly reduced pollution right around the toll plazas by allowing cars to drive straight through. Startlingly, the introduction of E-ZPass reduced the incidence of low birth weight by more than 10 percent in the neighborhoods nearest the toll plazas.

In another study, my collaborators and I examined birth records for 11 million newborns in five states. We found that a shocking 45 percent of mothers lived within about a mile of a site that emitted toxic chemicals such as heavy metals or organic carcinogens—a number that rose to 61 percent among Black mothers. Focusing on babies born to mothers who lived within a mile of a plant, we compared birth weights when the facility was operating with birth weights when it was closed. For additional context, we also compared babies born within a mile of a plant with babies born in a one-to-two-mile band around the plants. Both groups of mothers were likely to be similarly affected by the economics of factory openings and closings, but mothers who lived closer were more likely to have been exposed to pollution during pregnancy. We found that an operating plant increased the probability of low birth weight by 3 percent among babies whose mothers lived less than a mile from the plant.

The racial divide in pollution exposure is profound, in part because of continuing segregation in housing that makes it difficult for Black families to move out of historically Black neighborhoods. Disadvantaged communities may also lack the political power to fend off harmful development, such as a chemical plant, in their vicinity. In the E-ZPass study, roughly half of the mothers who lived next to toll plazas were Hispanic or Black, compared with only about a tenth of mothers who lived more than six miles away from a toll plaza. And in a paper published in 2020, John Voorheis of the U.S. Census Bureau, Walker and I showed that across the entire U.S., neighborhoods with higher numbers of Black residents have systematically worse air quality than other neighborhoods. Black people are also twice as likely as others to live near a Superfund hazardous waste site. For these reasons, pollution-control measures such as the Clean Air Act have greatly benefited Black people.

Fight or Flight

Stress disproportionately impacts the poor—who have chronic worries about paying bills, for example—and also harms fetuses. A stressful situation triggers the release of hormones that orchestrate a range of physical changes associated with the fight-or-flight response. Some of these hormones, including cortisol, have been linked to preterm labor, which in turn leads to low birth weight. High circulating levels of cortisol in the mother during pregnancy may damage the fetus's cortisol-regulation system, making it more vulnerable to stress. And stress can trigger behavioral responses in a mother such as increased smoking or drinking, which are also harmful to the fetus.

One revealing study indicates that fetal exposure to maternal stress can have greater negative long-term effects on mental health than stress directly experienced by a child. Petra Persson and Maya Rossin-Slater, both at Stanford University, looked at the impact of the death of a close relative. Death can bring many unwelcome changes to a family, such as reduced income, which may also influence child development. To account for such complications, the researchers used administrative data from Sweden to compare children whose mothers were affected by a death during the prenatal period with those whose mothers were affected by a death during the child's early years. They found that children affected by a death prenatally were 23 percent more likely to use medication for ADHD at ages nine to 11 and 9 percent more likely to use antidepressants in adulthood than were children whose families experienced a death a few years after their birth.

Another pathbreaking study measured levels of cortisol, an indicator of stress, during pregnancy. By age seven, children whose mothers had higher cortisol levels during pregnancy had received up to one year less schooling than their own siblings, indicating that they had been delayed in starting school. Moreover, for any given level of cortisol in the mother's blood, the negative effects were more pronounced for children born to less educated mothers. This finding suggests that although being stressed during pregnancy is damaging to the fetus, mothers with more education are better able to buffer the effects on their children—an important finding in view of the severe stress imposed by COVID on families today.

It is no surprise that disease can also harm a fetus. Douglas V. Almond of Columbia University looked at people born in the U.S. at the peak of the influenza epidemic of 1918 and found that they were 1.5 times more likely to be poor as adults than were those born just before them. In work I conducted with Almond and Mariesa Herrmann of Mathematica looking at mothers born between 1960 and 1990 in the U.S., we found that women who were born in areas where an infectious disease was raging were more likely to have diabetes when they gave birth to their own children decades later—and the effects were twice as large for Black people. More recently, Hannes Schwandt of Northwestern University examined Danish data and found that maternal infection with ordinary seasonal influenza in the third trimester doubles the rate of premature birth and low birth weight, and infection in the second trimester leads to a 9 percent reduction in earnings and a 35 percent increase in welfare dependence once the child reaches adulthood.

Preventing Harm

Health at birth and beyond can nonetheless be improved through thoughtful interventions targeting pregnant women, babies and children and through reductions in pollution. The food safety net in the U.S. has already had tremendous success in preventing low birth weight in the babies of disadvantaged women. The rollout of the food stamp program (now called the Supplemental Nutrition Assistance Program, or SNAP) across the U.S. in the mid-1970s reduced the incidence of low birth weight by between 5 and 11 percent. In addition, children who benefited from the rollout grew up to be less likely to have metabolic syndrome—a cluster of conditions that include obesity and diabetes. Notably, women who had benefited as fetuses or young children were more likely to be economically self-sufficient.

The 1970s also saw the introduction of the Special Supplemental Nutrition Program for Women, Infants and Children, popularly known as WIC. Approximately half of eligible pregnant women in the U.S. receive nutritious food from WIC, along with nutrition counseling and improved access to medical care. Dozens of studies have shown that when women participate in WIC during pregnancy, their babies are less likely to have low birth weight. In work looking at mothers in South Carolina, Anna Chorniy of Northwestern University, Lyudmyla Ardan (Sonchak) of Susquehanna University and I were able to show that children whose mothers received WIC during pregnancy were also less likely to have ADHD and other mental health conditions that are commonly diagnosed in early childhood.

In the late 1980s and early 1990s, state and federal governments worked together to greatly expand public health insurance for pregnant women under the Medicaid program. In work with Jonathan Gruber of the Massachusetts Institute of Technology, I showed that public health insurance lowered infant mortality and improved birth weight. Today the children whose mothers became eligible for health insurance coverage of their pregnancies in that period have higher levels of college attendance, employment and earnings than the children of mothers who did not. They also have lower rates of chronic conditions and are less likely to have been hospitalized. The estimated effects are strongest for Black people, who, having lower average incomes, benefited the most from the expansions. The fact that these babies are more likely to eventually get a college education also increases the life chances of their children. In the U.S., an additional year of college education for the mother reduces the incidence of low birth weight in her children by 10 percent.

Even so, too many children are still born with low birth weight, especially if their mothers are Black. Significantly, targeted interventions after birth can improve their outcomes. Programs such as the Nurse-Family Partnership provide home visits by nurses to low-income women who are pregnant for the first time, many of whom are young and unmarried. The nurse visits every month during the pregnancy and for the first two years of the child's life to provide guidance about healthy behavior. The assistance reduces child abuse and adolescent crime and enhances children's academic achievement.

Providing cash payments to poor families with young children also improves both maternal health and child outcomes, suggesting that COVID relief payments will have important protective effects. In the U.S., the largest preexisting program of this type is the Earned Income Tax Credit (EITC). Studies of beneficiaries of the EITC show that children in families that received increased amounts had higher test scores in school. With financial stress being somewhat relieved, the mental health of mothers in these families also improved. In addition, quality early-childhood education programs augment future health, education and earnings and reduce crime. Head Start, the federally funded preschool program that was rolled out beginning in the 1960s, has also had substantial positive effects on health and education outcomes, especially in places with less access to alternative child care centers.

A 2018 study, especially noteworthy in light of the tragic lead poisoning in Flint, Mich., shows that even some of the negative effects of lead can be reversed. In Charlotte, N.C., lead-poisoned children who received lead remediation, nutritional and medical assessments, WIC and special training for their caregivers saw reductions in problem behaviors and advanced school performance.

Looking Ahead

Investments in pregnant women and infants have been paying off, their success reflected in dramatically falling infant mortality rates in the U.S.–despite rising inequality in income and wealth. Alarmingly, however, many successful programs, such as the Clean Air Act, SNAP and Medicaid, are under attack. The Coronavirus Aid, Relief and Economic Security (CARES) Act passed in March 2020 provided some relief, at least with respect to Medicaid. CARES temporarily suspended disenrollment from the program, giving additional flexibility to state Medicaid programs in terms of time lines and eligibility procedures. Still, states may be hard-pressed to enroll the many who will become newly eligible for Medicaid because of job loss. Moreover, states that have not expanded the Medicaid program to cover otherwise ineligible low-income adults, as allowed by the Affordable Care Act, may see many more uninsured.

A National Academies of Sciences, Engineering and Medicine report published in 2019 laid out a road map for reducing child poverty by half within 10 years. One of the most stunning findings of the report is that it is feasible to meet that target by expanding programs that already exist. Following these directions would have a profound impact on health and health disparities. Targeted approaches, such as more thorough investigation of maternal deaths occurring up to one year after a birth, are also necessary. Even simple preventive measures such as giving pregnant women flu shots can have a tremendously positive effect on infant health and child development. Diagnosis and treatment of conditions such as preeclampsia (high blood pressure associated with pregnancy) are key to both protecting babies and lowering maternal mortality rates. It is important to help pregnant women quit smoking and to develop new approaches relevant to a new generation addicted to vaping. Also needed are stronger protections for women at risk of domestic violence, which leads directly to chronic stress, premature deliveries and low birth weight.

One salient open question is what effect the pandemic will have on the generation of children affected by it in utero and in early life. COVID itself may have negative effects on the developing fetus. The latest data suggest that although the overall risk is low, pregnant women are at increased risk of becoming critically ill (as they are with influenza or SARS). Affected babies, however, do not seem to be at risk of obvious birth defects (as they are with the Zika virus). Still, given the fact that COVID affects many body systems, it may prove to have subtler negative effects on the developing fetus. The pandemic is also an extremely stressful event compounded by the sharpest economic downturn since the Great Depression. There are reports of increases in domestic violence, alcohol consumption and drug overdoses, all of which are known to be harmful to the developing fetus. In consequence, the generation now in utero is likely to be at increased risk going forward and will require intensive social investments to overcome its poorer start in life.

In a recent sermon on the late civil rights leader John Robert Lewis, Reverend James Lawson recounted the significant gains for Americans of all colors that had resulted from that movement. He went on to ask that America's political leaders "work unfalteringly on behalf of every boy and every girl, so that every baby born on these shores will have access to the tree of life ... let all the people of the U.S.A. determine that we will not be quiet as long as any child dies in the first year of life in the United States. We will not be quiet as long as the largest poverty group in our nation are women and children." As we rebuild our shattered safety nets and public health systems in the aftermath of COVID-19, we need to seize the moment and use the knowledge we have gained about how to protect mothers and babies—to give every child the opportunity to flourish.

About the Author

Janet Currie is the Henry Putnam Professor of Economics and Public Affairs and co-director of the Center for Health and Wellbeing at Princeton University. She studies socioeconomic differences in health and access to health care, as well as environmental threats to health.

How Doctors Can Confront Racial Bias in Medicine

By Rachel Pearson

Medicine has a race problem. Doctors consistently provide worse care to people of color, particularly African-Americans and Latinos. In studies that control for socioeconomic status and access to care, researchers have found racial disparities in the quality of care across a wide range of diseases: asthma, heart attack, diabetes and prenatal care, to name a few. Two studies performed in emergency rooms showed that doctors were far more likely to fail to order pain medication for black and Hispanic patients who came in with bone fractures. Doctors are less likely to diagnose black patients with depression yet more likely to diagnose psychotic disorders such as schizophrenia. Hispanic HIV patients are twice as likely to die as white HIV patients, and black HIV patients are less likely to get antibiotics to prevent pneumonia. There is, however, one procedure that doctors are more likely to perform on black patients: amputation.

As a medical humanities M.D./Ph.D. student, I set out to understand how my profession, which prides itself on objectivity, could be influenced by something so subjective and harmful as racial bias. I found part of the answer in the kind of objectivity that doctors value. As trainees, we aspire to be like scientists, who see the self as a potential source of error and therefore try to suppress it. But medicine is not a science—it is a moral practice that uses science. When problematic parts of ourselves, such as racial bias, intrude, we find it hard to recognize the problem.

In studying memoirs of medical students and residents, I found that many trainees feel an acute anxiety about the self. When we react emotionally to intense situations, we worry that we are not being good doctors. When we do not react—when we coolly watch a patient die or approach a critically ill child with clinical detachment—we

Confronting Racism

worry that we are becoming monsters. We are unsure of the role emotions should play in clinical care. Interestingly, one specific emotion—discomfort—is thought to underlie disparities in care. Feeling uncomfortable, we rush out of encounters with patients of other races.

I was surprised to find that white trainees rarely mentioned race in their memoirs, even though we are disproportionately likely to care for patients of color in the free clinics and public hospitals where we learn. In medical school, we come to see race as a biological fact: something that predisposes certain patients to certain diseases. Medical students and residents of color perceive race differently—as a social experience. Former U.S. surgeon general Joycelyn Elders recounts being barred from the cafeteria when she was in medical school, and internist Rameck Hunt relates being unjustly arrested when he was a first-year med student. Navajo surgeon Lori Arviso Alvord writes about how touching a dead body in an anatomy lab course violates a Navajo taboo. Students of color also report feeling profoundly supported by their communities, and many are inspired by their own experiences of prejudice to provide excellent care to patients of color.

If white medical trainees avoid talking about race except as a biological fact, how can we explore racial bias? We might begin by revising our model of objectivity. Doctors are always themselves—emotional, particular and sometimes biased—in the hospital. We should accept this fact and learn to work with it. We should train ourselves, for example, to notice our own discomfort and respond by slowing down instead of rushing out of patient encounters. (Some medical schools are now training students to do just that.)

Other commonsense measures to tackle bias in care include aggressively recruiting and retaining medical students who reflect the diversity of the nation, explicitly training physicians to recognize unconscious bias and fairly promoting physicians of color within academic medicine. Ultimately, however, I hope that revising our understanding of objectivity in medicine can do more than just address bias. Medicine could be—it should be—a tool for ensuring that all people's lives are cherished. If we doctors begin to earn our authority as science-using moral leaders, then both medicine and society have much to gain.

About the Author

Rachel Pearson, M.D., Ph.D., graduated from the Institute for the Medical Humanities and the University of Texas Medical Branch. For five years she volunteered at and directed one of the largest student-run free clinics in the country. Her book No Apparent Distress *was published in 2017 by W. W. Norton.*

To Achieve Mental Health Equity, Dismantle Social Injustice

By Ruth S. Shim and Sarah Y. Vinson

In her book *Mediocre: The Dangerous Legacy of White Male America*, Ijeoma Oluo describes a phrase that she and her fellow social justice advocates use whenever injustice occurs in society: "works according to design," meaning that our unequal society didn't come about by accident—it was designed to keep historically marginalized people on the margins. Oluo uses the example of the many unarmed Black people killed by the police, while the perpetrators consistently avoid criminal trials. We recently observed this system at work with the differential law enforcement response to the attack of mostly white insurrectionists on the Capitol building compared to the crackdown on Black Lives Matter protesters last year.

As two Black women psychiatrists, in a field in which just 2 percent of all psychiatrists are black, we are repeatedly confronted with a disturbing trend in how the mental health system in the United States works. A majority of Black and Latinx adults with mental health problems do not have access to treatment, and almost 90 percent of Black and Latinx adults who have substance use disorders in the U.S. do not have access to effective care. Indigenous populations have higher rates of alcohol use disorder than other populations, and Black people are more likely to be diagnosed with schizophrenia, labeled as hostile and loaded up on high doses of antipsychotic medication than white people. Transgender youth have higher rates of suicide than cisgender youth. The list of inequities in mental health goes on and on.

More disturbing are the traditional explanations for why these inequities exist in the first place. In medical school, training and ongoing clinical practice, there is an emphasis on *biological determinism*, the false belief that people of different racial and ethnic groups are biologically and genetically different, and *cultural determinism*, the false belief that differences in health outcomes are the result of people's different cultural backgrounds and life choices. We (and our colleagues in medicine and other health professions) were taught to blame oppressed patients for their poor outcomes by implying inferiority (either biological or cultural) to the dominant white, straight, male culture, and that these poor outcomes were the result of incapability of oppressed and minoritized populations to conform to the standards of the dominant class and culture.

This type of argument persists today, with leading scholars advancing this argument as recently as July 2020. As members of groups most often oppressed—and members of the "untouchable" caste in the United States—we were faced with a cruel dilemma. To unpack what drives inequitable outcomes in health and mental health, either we must accept that we ourselves were members of a biologically and genetically inferior population—or come to a different conclusion, one in which we began to understand that the mental health system in the U.S. *works according to design* and is failing everyone in the process.

As we set out to review the evidence to support our hypothesis, data point after data point coalesced around a clear theme: the mental health of American society, particularly its marginalized members, is ravaged by the intentional, avoidable, inequitable distribution of resources, opportunities and basic protections. The most valuable framework for understanding the poor mental health outcomes and mental health inequities in this country is one of social injustice.

We also experienced the very personal manifestations of social injustice on mental health firsthand. While on a work retreat in San Miguel de Allende, Mexico (a city named in part after a prominent figure in Mexico's War of Independence), we took a guided *tacos and tequila* tour during one of our breaks, led by a friendly Latinx male in his early twenties. Despite the city's namesake, the young man defaulted to telling the city's story from the colonizer's perspective rather than that of the oppressed Indigenous people or the victorious revolutionaries.

Primed by the purpose of our trip and the work of the day, we asked the tour guide to give us the landmarks' *real* stories. Perhaps we wore him down over time, because, to our surprise, not only did he educate us about historic injustices in San Miguel de Allende, but also about his personal story of contemporary injustice he experienced in our home country of the United States.

After his birth in Mexico, our amiable tour guide had been brought to the United States by his parents at a very young age. The U.S. was his home, where he learned with his classmates, played soccer with his neighbors and formed childhood memories with his family—until he was detained for lack of proof of citizenship following a routine traffic stop. Unsure of whether he qualified for the Development, Relief, and Education for Alien Minors (DREAM) Act, and without the money for an immigration attorney, he and his loved ones had never explored his eligibility. He was routed to a detention facility and eventually deported. While he had some extended family in Mexico, the grief of losing the only home he had ever known, coupled with the trauma of his incarceration, bred despair.

The result: self-medication with crystal methamphetamine—the use of which quickly shifted to a substance use disorder. His recovery, while difficult, ushered in a realization of how great the fear of deportation had impacted his and his family's thoughts, feelings and behaviors—in essence, their mental health. He shared with us the relentless terror that was a way of life for himself and his family members and friends while living in the U.S.: fear of being stopped by the police, fear of being detained and deported—a constant level of anxiety that would meet all *Diagnostic and Statistical Manual of Mental Disorders (DSM-5)* criteria for generalized anxiety disorder.

Despite practicing as psychiatrists for many years in the U.S., neither of us had ever been taught to consider, or had ever seen, these patients who live in the shadows, living small, undetectable lives, in ceaseless terror of discovery. The shock of his story jolted us into a renewed desire to speak on behalf of these many never-to-be patients, who have been oppressed and marginalized by unjust and unfair policies in the U.S. that have impacted their mental

Section 2: Racism in Health and Psychology

health and increased the likelihood that they will develop substance use disorders as the only effective tool to cope with an unbearable burden of stress.

Six months later, we found ourselves submerged in the most dramatic manifestations of American injustice in our lifetimes. The COVID-19 pandemic took lives along the fault lines of chronic, intergenerational health, employment and socioeconomic racial inequities—killing people who looked like us, and like our siblings, our parents, and grandparents, at a rate of 3.6 times that for white people.

A few months into the pandemic, on a national holiday for those who died defending our nation and its freedoms, George Floyd died with a police officer's knee on his neck. Though he was neither the first nor the last unarmed Black person in police custody to take his last breath on video, George Floyd's final moments were broadcast to a nation slowed by COVID-19, and, perhaps, one also made acutely aware of the life and death implications of societal injustices.

After the extremely difficult year that was 2020, the evidence is compelling and overwhelming. The mental health system works according to design. As mental health professionals, we have failed in our most basic duties, and yet, many psychiatrists and other mental health professionals continue to display a disturbing lack of awareness of the role of social injustice in poor mental health and substance use disorder outcomes.

In a recent poll of members of the American Psychiatric Association (APA), when asked, "What are the top three ways that institutional racism is reflected in the APA as an organization, the second most common response was "none," meaning that a significant number of psychiatrists do not "see" institutional racism at the APA. These very psychiatrists care for oppressed and marginalized patients who are the victims of structural racism as a way of life. Furthermore, the medical community as a whole has also recently demonstrated that many physicians have a long way to go in understanding the role of structural racism on health outcomes in the U.S.

Professional negligence as it relates to social injustice is unacceptable. Social injustice is far too pervasive. It is far too impactful. The lives—and the psyches—of those we claim to serve are shared by oppression and injustice, which create the underlying context that drives the social determinants of health. Thus far, we have not operated with an understanding of how social injustice sets this context. To begin to make progress, the mental health system must transform to dismantle the underlying structural forces of racism, sexism, oppression and discrimination, and must support the advancement of policies and practices that promote justice and equity in mental health access and care. This requires leaders who are committed to making decisions that emphasize equity over profits, guided by the expertise of local communities and members of oppressed and marginalized communities. We do not have time to waste. Recent events must spur us to action. As writer and activist Angela Davis once said, "I am no longer accepting the things I cannot change, I'm changing the things I cannot accept."

This is an opinion and analysis article.

About the Authors

Ruth S. Shim, M.D., M.P.H., is the Luke & Grace Kim Professor in Cultural Psychiatry and a professor of clinical psychiatry in the Department of Psychiatry and Behavioral Sciences at the University of California, Davis.

Sarah Y. Vinson, M.D., is founder and principal consultant of Lorio Forensics and associate professor of psychiatry and pediatrics at Morehouse School of Medicine.

The authors are co-editors of the book Social (In)Justice and Mental Health *(American Psychiatric Association Publishing, 2021).*

Why Racism, Not Race, Is a Risk Factor for Dying of COVID-19

By Claudia Wallis

COVID-19 has cut a jarring and unequal path across the U.S. The disease has disproportionately harmed and killed people of color. Compared with non-Hispanic white people, American Indian, Black and Latinx individuals, respectively, faced 3.5, 2.8 and 3.0 times the risk of being hospitalized for the infection and 2.4, 1.9 and 2.3 times the chance of dying, according to the Centers for Disease Control and Prevention.

The reason for these disparities is not biological but is the result of the deep-rooted and pervasive impacts of racism, says epidemiologist and family physician Camara Phyllis Jones. Racism, she explains, has led people of color to be more exposed and less protected from the virus and has burdened them with chronic diseases. For 14 years Jones worked at the CDC as a medical officer and director of research on health inequities. As president of the American Public Health Association in 2016, she led a campaign to explicitly name racism as a direct threat to public health. She is currently a Presidential Visiting Fellow at the Yale School of Medicine and is writing a book proposing strategies for a national campaign against racism.

As the country began to confront the unequal impact of COVID and the ongoing legacy of racial injustice it represents, Jones spoke with *Scientific American* contributing editor Claudia Wallis about the ways that discrimination has shaped the suffering produced by the pandemic.

Along with age, male gender and certain chronic conditions, race has turned out to be a risk factor for a severe outcome from COVID. Why is that?

Race doesn't put you at higher risk. Racism puts you at higher risk. It does so through two mechanisms: People of color are more infected because we are more exposed and less protected. Then, once infected, we are more likely to die because we carry a greater burden of chronic diseases from living in disinvested communities with poor food options [and] poisoned air and because we have less access to health care.

Why do you say Black, brown and Indigenous people are more exposed?

We are more exposed because of the kinds of jobs that we have: the frontline jobs of home health aides, postal workers, warehouse workers, meat packers, hospital orderlies. And those frontline jobs—which, for a long time, have been invisibilized and undervalued in terms of the pay—are now categorized as essential work. The overrepresentation [of people of color] in these jobs doesn't just so happen. (Nothing differential by race just so happens.) It is tied to residential and educational segregation in this country. If you have a poor neighborhood, then you'll have poorly funded schools, which often results in poor education outcomes and another generation lost. When you have poor educational outcomes, you have limited employment opportunities.

We are also more exposed because we are overrepresented in prisons and jails—jails where people are often financial detainees because they can't make bail. And brown people are more exposed in immigration detention centers. We are also more likely to be unhoused—with no access to water to wash our hands—or to live in smaller, more cramped quarters in more densely populated neighborhoods. You're in a one-bedroom apartment with five people living there, and one is your grandmother, and you can't safely isolate from family members who are frontline workers.

Why have people of color been less protected?

We have been less protected because in these frontline jobs—but also in the nursing homes and in the jails, prisons and homeless shelters—the personal protective equipment [PPE] was very, very slow in coming. Look at the meatpacking plants, for example. We are less protected because our roles and our lives are less valued—less valued in our job roles, less valued in our intellect and our humanity.

You've noted that once infected, people of color are more likely to have a poor outcome or die. Could you break down the reasons?

This has two buckets: First, we are more burdened with chronic diseases. Black people have 60 percent more diabetes and 40 percent more hypertension. That's not because we are not interested in health but because of the context of our lives. We are living in unhealthier places without the food choices we need: no grocery stores, so-called food deserts and what some people describe as "fast-food swamps." More polluted air, no place to exercise safely, toxic dump sites—all of these things go into communities that have been disempowered. That's why we have more diseases, not because we don't want to be healthy. We very much want to be healthy. It's because of the burdens that racism has put on our bodies.

What is the second bucket that raises risks from COVID?

Health care. Even from the beginning, it was hard for Black folks to get tested because of where testing sites were initially located. They were in more affluent neighborhoods—or there was drive-through testing. What if you don't have a car? And there was the need to have a physician's order to get a test. We heard about people who were symptomatic and presented at emergency departments but were sent back home without getting a test. A lot of people died at home without ever having a confirmed diagnosis. So even though we know we are overrepresented, we may have been undercounted.

Once you get into the hospital, there's a whole spectrum of scarce resources, so different states and hospital systems had what they called "crisis standards of care." In Massachusetts, they were very careful to say you cannot use race or language or zip code to discriminate [on who gets a ventilator]. But you could use expected [long-term] survival. Then the question was: Do you have these preexisting conditions? This was going to systematically put Black and brown people at a lower priority or even disqualify them from access to these lifesaving therapies. [Editor's Note: Massachusetts later changed its guidelines, but Jones viewed the revision as an incomplete fix.]

Making sure that vaccine campaigns reach communities of color is surely part of the solution, but what else can be done to better protect vulnerable minorities?

We need more PPE for all frontline workers; we need to value all those lives. We need to offer hazard pay and something like conscientious objector status for frontline workers who feel it is too dangerous to go back into the poultry or meatpacking plant. We know there are communities at higher risk, and we need to be doing more testing there. We need to broaden our gaze from a narrow focus on the individual ("vaccine hesitancy") to acknowledge that structural barriers continue to impact access to the vaccines.

Several states do not report racial and ethnic data on COVID cases. Why is that a problem?

States should be reporting their data disaggregated by race, especially now we know Black and brown and Indigenous folks are at higher risk of being infected and then dying. It's not just to document it, not just to alarm or to arm some people with a false sense of security. It's because we need to provide resources according to need: healthcare resources, testing resources and prevention types of resources.

Are you concerned about how the CDC's relaxation of its face mask guidance will impact essential workers and communities of color?

Yes. We need to recognize that we are all in this together, that masks provide reciprocal protection with no downsides, and that asymptomatic spread continues to fuel this pandemic, so that a continued mask mandate for all without regard to immunization status should be maintained until there are no COVID infections, hospitalizations or deaths. It is such a simple, effective, and community-minded intervention that hurts no one and helps everyone.

Over the past year we have seen people take to streets to protest another kind of deadly racial inequity: police violence against people of color, especially against Black men and boys. As awareness spreads about the pervasive nature of racism in systems ranging from law enforcement to health care to housing, do you see an opportunity for meaningful change?

The outrage is encouraging because it has been expressed by folks from all parts of our population. The Black Lives Matter protests were potentially mixing bowls for the virus, but at least they are not frivolous mixing bowls like pool parties. Participants in such protests were thinking not just about their individual health and well-being but about the collective power they have now to possibly make things better for their children and grandchildren. This is both a treacherous time and a time of great promise.

Racism is a system of structuring opportunity and assigning value based on the social interpretation of how one looks (which is what we call "race") that unfairly disadvantages some individuals and communities, unfairly advantages other individuals and communities, and saps the strength of the whole society through the waste of human resources. Perhaps this nation is awakening to the realization that racism does indeed hurt us all.

About the Author

Claudia Wallis is an award-winning science journalist whose work has appeared in the New York Times, Time, Fortune *and the* New Republic. *She was science editor at* Time *and managing editor of* Scientific American Mind.

Teaching Antiracism to the Next Generation of Doctors

By Rupinder Kaur Legha

A psychotic Black woman admitted to a psychiatric emergency room is discharged "to the streets," despite being pregnant and disorganized. Several white health care providers, noting her history of methamphetamine use, joke "she's always like this" and claim she is "at baseline," suggesting she is inherently inferior and unworthy of treatment. They make no effort to contact her family, provide prenatal care or admit her to the hospital, carelessly disregarding the potential harm to her and her unborn child.

When two Black parents refuse a potentially life-saving organ transplant for their child, the pediatricians consider reporting them to child protective services for neglect. The pediatricians themselves neglect to fully explain the complex medical details to the terrified parents. Only when a consulting psychiatric service recognizes the parents' legitimate fears and the absence of appropriate education do the pediatricians refocus on improving medical care, rather than reporting.

In neither case is the providers' medical racism challenged, sanctioned or remediated.

As a physician-educator teaching about racism, my primary goal is ensuring the next generation of doctors never engages in this kind of discrimination, which is common within the American health care system.

Unfortunately, existing medical education pedagogies, such as the social determinants of health and cultural competency, do not challenge the racism perpetuated by a predominantly white health care work force charged with caring for a racially diverse public they do not represent. They are increasingly out of sync with the demands for antiracism following the murders of Ahmaud Arbery, George

Section 2: Racism in Health and Psychology

Floyd and Breonna Taylor and the coronavirus's disproportionate killing of Black lives.

Instead, I teach an antiracist approach informed by Ibram Kendi's scholarship that helps students identify racism's far-reaching grasp on health care so they can challenge it and honor their oath to first do no harm. Rather than master a competency, I invite them to begin a lifelong journey intended to excavate the racism, anti-Blackness and white supremacy shaping their profession, their country, and themselves.

Learning the legacy of slavery in American medicine is key to this process. To echo a recent *New England Journal of Medicine* editorial, "Slavery has produced a legacy of racism, injustice, and brutality that runs from 1619 to the present, and that legacy infects medicine as it does all social institutions." Ta-Nehisi Coates' ethical, legal and economic justification for reparations and Carol Anderson's discussion of the white rage pushing back on Black economic and civic advancement are not typical medical education content. But because they elucidate slavery's long arc in American history and render parallel arcs in American medicine more visible and less refutable, they are requisite teaching.

My students learn that when health care providers claim a psychotic pregnant Black woman is "just like that" or "at baseline" and discharge her to the streets with no plan for shelter, they are advancing the same narrative of Black mental inferiority and physical imperviousness to harm that 19th-century doctors used to justify slavery. When they report Black families to family services as a form of coercion, in lieu of offering the standard of care by providing education, they are pathologizing their suffering and disregarding their historical mistreatment by the health care system. Failing to hospitalize a medically acute Black pregnant woman is not only negligent. It upholds the assault on Black women's reproductive health foundational to slavery, maintained through forced-sterilization campaigns lasting into the 1970s, and enduring in their higher risk for maternal mortality today.

Recognizing the legacy of slavery in American medicine enables students to discern contemporary racism. It simultaneously elucidates why, as a *Lancet* editorial recently stated, "Racism is a public health emergency of global concern. It is the root cause of continued disparities in death and disease between Black and white people in the USA."

But challenging racism's deleterious effects requires first identifying its many forms. Camara Phyllis Jones' classic multilevel framework emphasizes how racism is internalized, operates interpersonally through implicit bias and microaggressions, and functions on more macro levels through institutions, policies and ideologies. Racism's multiple levels can powerfully collide, resulting in dangerous clinical "care." Using this model, students learn why microaggressions, such as ignoring a patient's subjective complaint of shortness of breath, are anything but "micro" and can, in fact, be deadly when they intersect with the health care system's inadequacies. All this must be understood against a background of white supremacy that has lynched and massacred countless Black Americans. Accordingly, white doctors' silence when white patients hurl racial slurs at their Black colleagues is equally damaging to health.

They also learn how racist policies and ideologies operating outside of health care influence clinical interactions. The War on Drugs, fabricated in the 1970s to push back on Black advancement from the Civil Rights Movement, was reinforced by an ideology of Black criminality and violence perpetuated, in part, by American psychiatrists. Doctors, no less immune to these racist ideologies, are equally prone to the disproportionate punishment and policing of Black lives well-documented in school and law enforcement settings. Common clinical practices, like administering forced intramuscular medication, discharging someone who should be hospitalized, or reporting a family to family services, become coercive when the racism driving them proceeds unchecked.

The ostensible scientific neutrality of clinical decision-making can obfuscate the racism that leads doctors to misdiagnose, deny treatment, silence subjective complaints and pathologize emotional responses. However, recognizing slavery's legacy and racism's multiple levels renders such bias more visible, preparing students to engage in antiracist clinical care. I ask them to disavow the prevailing medical culture that encourages perfection and, instead, admit to being racist in order to become antiracist.

Challenging racism's multiple levels and historical arcs is an established antiracist approach but not a common one in medical education. My best hope is that in the absence of broader accountability from the health care system, this kind of education will not only prevent students from participating in the clinical racism I described earlier. It will provide shared language for them to collectively speak out and heighten their conscience and consciousness enough so they first do no harm.

Unfortunately, the next generation of doctors is training within a health care system steeped in racism. They are demanding antiracist medical education from majority-white faculty unequipped to train them. The white fragility of academic medicine, which is dominated by white male leadership, may impede meaningful antiracist educational reform. Furthermore, there are few effective outlets for reporting discrimination and remediating it. As students become more familiar with antiracist pedagogy, they are bound to report racism at academic medical centers more frequently. The process is likely to be contentious. Following an incident during a lecture on gender-based violence at the University of Washington School of Medicine, for example, a coalition of Black students recently called for the removal of three professors for "anti-Black, racist" behavior.

If my recent discussions are any indication, the next generation of doctors is primed to name and identify the racism that stripped George Floyd of his life and to leverage the weight of their authority to protect rather than harm their patients. They are simultaneously seeking structural reforms to ensure sustained equality. The question is: Are the academic medical centers where they train prepared to teach them to do so?

About the Author

Rupinder Kaur Legha, M.D., is a child and adolescent psychiatrist in Los Angeles, California.

Section 3: Policing Race

3.1 A Civil Rights Expert Explains the Social Science of Police Racism
By Lydia Denworth and Alexis J. Hoag

3.2 How to Reduce Police Violence
By Dina Fine Maron

3.3 Police Violence Calls for Measures Beyond De-Escalation Training
By Stacey McKenna

3.4 I Can't Breathe: Asthma, Black Men and the Police
By Obasi Okorie, Ekemini Hogan and Utibe Effiong

A Civil Rights Expert Explains the Social Science of Police Racism

By Lydia Denworth and Alexis J. Hoag

In a now infamous event captured on video, on May 25, 2020, George Floyd, a 46-year-old Black man, was killed by a Minneapolis police officer outside of a corner store. Derek Chauvin kneeled on Floyd's neck for nine minutes and 29 seconds while two other officers helped to hold him down and a third stood guard nearby. Nearly a year later, in April 2021, a jury convicted Chauvin of second-degree murder, third-degree murder and second-degree manslaughter. He could face decades in prison (sentencing was expected on June 25). In a highly unusual development, other police officers, including the Minneapolis chief of police, testified against Chauvin.

The three other officers involved, Thomas Lane, J. Alexander Kueng and Tou Thao, were indicted on a range of state and federal charges, including violating Floyd's constitutional rights, failing to intervene to stop Chauvin, and aiding and abetting second-degree murder and second-degree manslaughter. Their trial is scheduled for March 2022.

The 2014 shooting death of Black teenager Michael Brown in Ferguson, Mo., sparked a renewed emphasis on racism and police brutality in the U.S.'s political and cultural conversation. In the past few years many names have been added to the list of Black people killed by police. Despite some efforts to acknowledge and grapple with systemic racism in American institutions, anger and distrust between law enforcement and Black Americans have remained high. But Floyd's death sparked a new level of outrage. Protests erupted in hundreds of cities around the U.S. in the summer of 2020. Most demonstrations were peaceful. But some turned violent, with police using force against protesters and a small percentage of people setting fire to police cars, looting stores, and defacing or damaging buildings. By July the demonstrations were thought to be the largest protest movement in American history, with some 15 million to 26 million people estimated to have taken part.

In addition to the criminal charges against the officers, Floyd's death has prompted U.S. Justice Department investigations into the practices of the Minneapolis Police Department. And Democrats in Congress are hoping to pass criminal justice reform legislation named for Floyd. Both reflect the interests of the new administration since Joe Biden took office in January 2021.

In June 2020, at the height of the protests, *Scientific American* spoke with civil rights attorney Alexis J. Hoag. Hoag is the inaugural practitioner in residence at the Eric H. Holder, Jr., Initiative for Civil and Political Rights at Columbia University. She works with both undergraduates and law school students at Columbia to introduce them to civil rights fieldwork (which she describes as "real issues, real clients, real cases"). Hoag was previously a senior counsel at the NAACP Legal Defense and Educational Fund. *Scientific American* asked her to share her perspective on the history that has brought the U.S. to a breaking point—and her ideas for how to make substantive improvements in how law enforcement and courts treat Black people in the country.

Why are we seeing this level of protest now?

I think it's a combination of things. COVID-19 [has had a] disproportionate impact on Black people because of long-standing structural inequalities. Black people are more likely to live in hypersegregated low-income areas that are underresourced. And Black people are more prone to the very preexisting conditions that make people vulnerable to COVID-19 because of structural inequality and lack of access to health care. We've all been cooped up for 10 to 11 weeks. Forty million people [in the U.S.] are unemployed. And there was something egregious about the video that circulated of George Floyd being executed for the suspicion of tendering a counterfeit $20 bill. And I want to stress "suspicion" because we still don't know. That became a death sentence for him.

The violence that has been rendered against Black bodies has gone on for centuries. Now it's out there for everyone to see. And the response, which is hopeful and heartening to me, is that people—not just Black Americans—in this country are really disturbed and appropriately so.

What are the important historical factors that have led up to this point?

I lean so heavily on the unique history of this country and the fact that we enslaved people, Black people. To hold people in bondage as property, you had to look at them as less than human. You see that continuing to happen today in [what] I refer to as the criminal legal system, not the justice system, because it is not just. We are not there yet. As an appellate attorney, I read a lot of transcripts of trials. And the level of dehumanization that prosecutors use to refer to Black criminal defendants is striking. It's the verbiage used, that the defendant was "circling" and "hunting" the victim. What hunts and circles? Animals. When you can dehumanize an individual, of course, you can put the person away for a long time, you can sentence him or her to death. And of course, you can put your knee on somebody's neck for nine minutes because you see them as less than human. It's a combination of the dehumanization of Black people with the presumption of dangerousness and criminality.

Is racism getting worse? Or has the ubiquity of cell phones and video recordings simply made us more aware of it?

These issues are getting amplified; they're getting recorded. I think back to the early 1990s and Rodney King's videotaped beating. That really galvanized people around this issue—an issue that many Black Americans were intimately aware of already—and put it out there for the world to see. Then the response after those officers were acquitted was public demonstrations in 1992 in Los Angeles. I think people would not have been as engaged if we didn't have that image. Now we walk around with [cameras] in our pockets.

Section 3: Policing Race

How does the seeming increase in white nationalism fit in?

I don't know that I would call it an increase. White nationalists, known earlier as white supremacists, first rallied [more than] 150 years ago to violently limit the freedom of newly emancipated Black Americans. Despite federal legislation extending the benefits of citizenship to Black people, white supremacists passed state laws codifying inequality and used violence and intimidation to curtail any Black exercise of freedom. What's happening now [in June 2020] is that we have [a presidential] administration that welcomes and encourages white nationalist views and activities.

Have events in Ferguson and other cities, and the Black Lives Matter movement as a whole, had any effect on policing?

Ferguson was a massive wake-up call. There was a brief glimmer of hope. There was a mechanism in place: the Law Enforcement Misconduct [Statute]. It [is] a federal law the Department of Justice could rely on to investigate Ferguson, to investigate police misconduct in Baltimore [where Freddie Gray, a 25-year-old Black man, died while being transported in a police vehicle in what was ruled to be a homicide]. That law was grossly underutilized by Attorney General William Barr. Who the administration is and who the chief law-enforcement officer of this country is—the attorney general of the U.S.—makes a difference. We've seen a massive rollback in the responsiveness of the [Trump] administration [in taking] a hard look at injustice and at rampant police misconduct.

The other step back that the country has taken is to characterize officers involved in misconduct as "a few bad apples." I think we all need to admit that it's not a few bad apples; it's a rotten apple tree. The history of policing in the South [was driven in part by] slave patrols that were monitoring the movement of Black bodies. And in the North, law enforcement was privately funded [and often involved protecting property and goods]. The police got started targeting poor people and Black people.

What would you like to see happen now?

I think there needs to be a really hard conversation nationally and within law enforcement. To use force, police officers have to reasonably believe that their lives are in danger. What is it about Black skin that makes law enforcement feel threatened for their lives? In addition, there are legal mechanisms that need to be examined. "Qualified immunity" as a defense to police misconduct was judicially created in 1982. It shields government officials from being sued for discretionary actions that are performed within their official capacities unless the action violates clearly established federal law. Somebody who is suing an officer for tasing someone while they're handcuffed has to find a case from the U.S. Supreme Court or the highest court of appeals in their jurisdiction that says that exact act—being handcuffed and tased—is unconstitutional. This is a massive hurdle for a plaintiff.

What are social scientists and researchers doing to help?

Data are currency. We can create a national database of officer misconduct. You have officers such as Derek Chauvin, who had 18 complaints against him and [was] still allowed to operate within the [Minneapolis Police] Department.

The data collection that happens within police departments enabled experts in the stop-and-frisk litigation [against] the [New York City Police Department] to shine a spotlight on gross disparities: the rate of stops and searches of Black and brown men and boys [coupled with] the low rate of actually acquiring contraband. They found that the rate of securing contraband from white individuals who had been stopped and frisked was so much higher because the police were actually using discretion.

There's powerful data collection that happens in our criminal courts. Studies show that, all factors being equal, judges are rendering longer and harsher sentences for Black defendants. These judges are setting higher bail. You can isolate all these other factors, but race is the difference. That's very powerful—to be able to document and publish those findings.

There has also been some really good social science research on implicit bias and the way that it operates. We could all take [implicit association tests] on our computers. You could do a training with your employees. To start with, there is this recognition, this acknowledgment, that we all have implicit bias.

And how do we use that information and not just let people off the hook?

Let's talk about it. Social science research shows that when there's recognition that we harbor implicit bias, that awareness can help mitigate [such] bias impacting our daily interactions and decisions.

What about people's decision to protest during the pandemic? Are you worried that protesters will get sick and spread COVID-19?

Of course. I worry that there will be a second wave of infections. But I think that also speaks to how pressing the issue is and how strongly people feel about it—that they are risking their lives to bring attention to the rampant and lethal mistreatment of Black and brown bodies at the hands of law enforcement.

About the Author

Lydia Denworth is a Brooklyn, N.Y.–based science writer, a contributing editor for Scientific American *and author of* Friendship: The Evolution, Biology, and Extraordinary Power of Life's Fundamental Bond *(W. W. Norton, 2020).*

How to Reduce Police Violence

By Dina Fine Maron

In the latest police shooting of an unarmed black man, an officer in North Miami this week shot Charles Kinsey—a therapist who was lying on the ground with his arms in the air. He had apparently been trying to help a patient with autism who was sitting in the street. Kinsey survived, but the incident follows lethal ones in Minnesota and Louisiana and the murders of eight officers in two states.

Police, policy makers and scientists are scrambling for answers about how to combat excessive—and often deadly—force against African-Americans. Many researchers say a first step might be to obtain better data on how often police departments use physical force against people, and under what circumstances. A think tank called the Center for Policing Equity this month published the strongest data yet on how often officers use force on the job and how those actions differ according to the race of the people involved. The data echo what is playing out in near-daily headlines: Across geographically and demographically diverse swaths of the country, physical force—via restraint, punches, tasers and guns—is disproportionately exerted against black people, even after taking into account differences for violent crime arrest rates and other factors.

That conclusion comes from data spanning the years 2010 to 2015, voluntarily provided by 12 police departments across the country. The identities of departments were kept anonymous in the report.

University of California, Berkeley's Jack Glaser, an expert on implicit racial bias among police and co-author of the new report, spoke with *Scientific American* about the Center's work, ways to confront bias, and the many questions that seem impossible to answer in a country stunned by the escalating violence.

An edited transcript of the interview follows.

We know that police officers, like the rest of us, can be subject to implicit bias. Can you briefly describe what that is?

Section 3: Policing Race

Implicit biases reflect positive or negative mental associations that people have between groups, like racial or ethnic groups, and specific traits like criminality or danger. They are implicit in the sense that they reside in the part of our memory that is not accessible to conscious introspection. They get activated in our memories when we encounter somebody from one of those groups or when we think about those groups. It's maladaptive when it causes us to make biased judgments about individuals based on prior conceptions about the groups they belong to.

Groups including your think tank, the Center for Policing Equity, have worked to design programs for police officers that aim to help combat implicit bias on the job. What does this training look like?

A lot of people are calling for implicit bias training, including Hillary Clinton. They typically look like lecture-based and discussion-based conversations about what implicit bias is, and how it influences your judgments and causes you to make discriminatory judgments.

Do we have actual data showing that this training changes officers' actions in the field?

Unfortunately none of them have been shown to have any actual impact on performance. You can raise people's awareness about the possibility that implicit bias exists and affects them, but that's not the same thing as stopping it from influencing their judgments. The nature of implicit bias is that you can't feel it operating. There are internal reports evaluating these programs, but they haven't been published in the peer-reviewed research. Generally, we are still working with very little information.

What the scientists will tell you is that you shouldn't be calling this "training" because you don't want to give people the impression that their behavior is being changed. It's raising awareness. It is possible that the process of talking about biases, if not done correctly, can reinforce them—or that when people believe they've been de-biased or trained they feel credentialed to go about their business without worrying about bias as much, which could actually increase bias.

So how do we get good data?

We are building this national justice database at CPE and are hoping to be able to look at the effects of these [implicit bias] trainings on actual performance outcomes. We don't have any existing comparable data across police departments. If you were going to test this within a department you would randomly assign some units to do it and compare their actions, but that hasn't been done. At best you get some explicit attitude change, but no implicit attitude change and no improvement in performance.

If implicit bias workshops may not be the answer, what can police departments do?

We don't know how to de-bias people because the culture is so saturated with those stereotypes. My general recommendation is— and I think it's consistent with what the Center for Policing Equity is generally proposing—that departments find ways to reduce the rates at which these interactions are occurring.

Meaning what?

Police have a lot of discretion on who they can engage with and who they detain, and that can result in wild variation in discretionary stops. You can reduce the amount of contacts without compromising public safety and then the chance for biased outcomes gets reduced dramatically. We have seen that in NYC: The number of stops are way down and the racial disparities are mathematically necessarily reduced because there is less room for disparity.

The 12 departments that gave you their data voluntarily were told that they would be kept anonymous. How do you know the data are accurate?

We are always concerned about the accuracy of self-reported data. Our hope is by keeping this anonymous we will hedge against that.

As the database gets bigger—we have many more lined up to join beyond these 12—we will see a large proportion of the U.S. population represented. My expectation is within a year or two we will, conservatively, have police departments covering half the U.S. population represented. We are targeting large departments. The concerns are still there about the accuracy of the data that is being reported. Some of them just send PDF files with summary statistics. We are working with all of these departments to collect raw data to be sent to us at the incident level but there is a lot of variation there.

This is the first public data on this issue. How did you make it happen?

CPE has been working for years now to build relationships with police departments, that's a big part of it. There is this existing relationship between CPE and some big city chiefs and some smaller towns too. We got a grant from the National Science Foundation and some additional funding from some private funders so we could pull together a team of researchers and staffers to make this happen. We have some retired police on staff who are doing this outreach. That's very helpful.

Any other good data-driven areas you are hopeful about to combat unnecessary use of force?

Community policing is an ill-defined concept and every police department will say they are doing it. To have good data on that you would need it to be comparable in areas where there is variation in style of policing, or areas where they are doing it versus not doing it. The national justice database is trying to get at part of that. It's hard to say what specifically works until we know who is doing what.

One thing I am enthusiastic about is the psychology of intergroup contact in policing. Mere contact with members of different groups—racial, ethnic, sexual orientation, ideological, national—as long as it's not negative, competitive contact, reduces bias toward other groups. There's been some great work on this that I hope we can inject into community-oriented policing.

About the Author

Dina Fine Maron, formerly an associate editor at Scientific American, *is now a wildlife trade investigative reporter at* National Geographic.

Police Violence Calls for Measures Beyond De-Escalation Training

By Stacey McKenna

Black people are about three times more likely than white people to be killed by a police officer. Outrage over this long-running and relentless situation boiled over in the summer of 2020, with people across the U.S. taking to the streets to protest the killings of George Floyd, Breonna Taylor, and so many others. The demonstrations—which themselves were largely peaceful—have involved notable incidents of police violence toward protesters. These events have further amplified questions about officers' use of force and one of the most popular strategies aimed at reducing it: de-escalation.

The 2014 police shooting of Michael Brown in Ferguson, Mo., and the surge of civil unrest that followed prompted then president Barack Obama to assemble the President's Task Force on 21st Century Policing. A resulting report called for nationwide changes in law enforcement, with the aim of promoting "effective crime reduction while building public trust." De-escalation was one strategy that subsequently gained many new followers.

Although the approach is widely employed to reduce violence and aggression in health care and mental health settings, its application for law enforcement is poorly defined. In a policing context, de-escalation aims to decrease the use of force against civilians by teaching officers techniques to slow things down and use time, space and communication to find an alternative—practices that run counter to much law-enforcement training. Police are traditionally taught to make decisions and act as quickly as possible. And they learn early on that society not only authorizes but sometimes expects them to use force as a means of coercion.

Unlike strategies that specifically target discrimination—from the racial sensitivity training adopted in the 1980s to more recent implicit bias training—de-escalation is touted by proponents as a means of reducing violence across the board. The approach, they say, protects civilians and officers alike and enables police to peacefully manage crowds of protesters.

De-escalation has become one of the types of training most frequently requested by police departments in recent years, says Robin Engel, a professor at the University of Cincinnati's School of Criminal Justice. A recent CBS News poll of 155 departments indicates that at least 71 percent of them offer some form of de-escalation training, although it is not always mandatory. But U.S. news outlets have reported numerous, often startling stories of police violence against individuals and groups of protesters across the country. Many departments in cities where such uses of force have taken place—including those in Seattle and Phoenix (neither of which responded to requests for comment)—require their officers to undergo training in de-escalation. So why does it often break down?

De-Escalation Is Not Enough

In 2016 Campaign Zero—a law-enforcement reform initiative developed by Black Lives Matter activists—helped to conduct an analysis of 91 police departments in the largest U.S. cities. The study found that de-escalation mandates were associated with lower rates of police killings and fewer officers being killed or assaulted in the line of duty—even after accounting for a number of departmental and social factors. Although a review of cross-disciplinary research on de-escalation found that such training probably has slight-to-moderate benefits and few drawbacks, much of the research has methodological weaknesses—including a lack of control groups, dependence on correlational designs and use of self-reporting rather than observation-based data. Thus, despite promising early findings, Engel argues that there is not yet enough systematic research about de-escalation in policing to show it is effective or to guide its use.

But what is increasingly clear, she says, is that even effective de-escalation training is probably an insufficient solution if it is used on its own. "We know that training alone doesn't change behavior," Engel says. "So you need a strong use-of-force policy that emphasizes the use of de-escalation tactics. And you need to couple that with accountability and supervisory oversight—and then add in the training component. Agencies that have been doing [these things] are [anecdotally] reporting success." Similarly, Campaign Zero reports that the departments with the lowest rates of police killings and officer deaths employed four or more of the organization's 8 Can't Wait strategies aimed at reducing the use of force. In addition to de-escalation mandates, this campaign calls for measures such as banning choke holds and changing how the use of force is reported.

Still, measures seeking to reduce the violence—or the unevenness in how it is carried out—without addressing its root cause may be seen as inauthentic. For example, law-enforcement officials in some cities have marched and knelt alongside protesters. Such actions—viewed by many as a show of solidarity—have served to de-escalate heated situations, but some question the sincerity of these gestures.

"De-escalation is a code word for pacification," says Christen Smith, an associate professor of anthropology and African and African diaspora studies at the University of Texas at Austin. "Policing in the Americas uses code words in order to try to frame violent actions as something less violent than what they really are," adds Smith, who researches state violence in the region, with focuses on Brazil and the U.S. She contends that calls for de-escalation training—especially in the absence of more comprehensive change—can be used as a political tool to "gift wrap violence in a prettier package" rather than a method to reconfigure the system to keep communities safe in ways that feel equitable.

What Works

Some activists and law-enforcement officials say it may be possible to change police departments—or the criminal justice system itself—to accomplish that goal. Indeed, the communities that have demonstrated success have taken a comprehensive approach to reducing police violence. The police department in Camden, N.J., for example, was disbanded and rebuilt with a new vision in 2013.

"We try to meet the community before anything is an emergency, before there is a crisis," says Camden police captain Zsakhiem R. James. "We partner with the community, so we're not seen as an occupying force." In addition to such engagement—which sometimes means hosting and attending barbecues and block parties—the department now has a strict and clear use-of-force policy, as well as extensive and ongoing training in de-escalation. This training includes scripts and virtual role-playing, along with thorough oversight procedures such as monitored body cameras, James says. What is more, he adds, the department has a deep commitment to this different approach to policing. "This entire department is community-based," he says. "If you can't abide by our policies, you just don't need to work here. People employed by us and working for us must abide by it."

This type of multipronged strategy to address state-authorized violence and change the face of policing in the U.S. has been gaining traction. Minneapolis has vowed to dismantle its own police department and replace it with a community-led alternative. And state and national lawmakers have introduced bills that would restrict the use of force, increase civilian oversight and develop tracking systems for officer misconduct. On June 3, 2020, the Law Enforcement Action Partnership (LEAP) released several recommendations to local, state and national officials that integrate immediate interventions (including de-escalation) aimed at reducing the use of force with system-wide accountability and steps toward structural change.

"Law enforcement is the dumping ground. When you don't know who to call, you call the cops," says former police officer Kyle Kazan, who is now a speaker for LEAP. "You have to take a step back and ask, 'What does society need law enforcement for?' We need to rethink how we handle society's challenges." He argues that ending the War on Drugs, increasing funding for dedicated social workers and outreach workers, and ensuring that officers are held liable for their actions within and across departments would better position law enforcement to help communities.

Such interventions, as well as the movement to defund the police, start to address one of Smith's major critiques of a reformist approach that stops at training. "There's a deep-rooted connection between the way that we understand justice in this country, white supremacy and anti-Blackness," she says, noting that modern policing in the U.S. grew, in part, out of slave patrols in the South. "How do you undo that culture? As anthropologists, we know that the only way cultures die is when they disappear into history because of some catastrophic event [such as the collapse of a nation or descent into civil war]. What our generation is tasked with is trying to figure out a way to dismantle this culture without a catastrophic event."

About the Author

Stacey McKenna is a medical anthropologist and freelance journalist who writes about science, travel and all things equine.

I Can't Breathe: Asthma, Black Men and the Police

By Obasi Okorie, Ekemini Hogan and Utibe Effiong

In late September, a New York Supreme Court judge ordered a judicial inquiry into the death of Eric Garner. In 2014, Garner's last words, "I can't breathe," caught on tape, became a national rally cry for criminal justice reform in the United States. Those same words have been spoken by many Black men during their last moments of life while interacting with the police.

It has been known for centuries that Black men are more likely to die in police custody than men of other races. Could there be other factors aside from the color of their skin that puts these men at risk? Because "I can't breathe" is so frequently uttered, one such factor could be asthma.

Asthma, also known as bronchial asthma, is a chronic disease of the airway characterized by intermittent inflammation of the airways, which over time leads to irreversible changes. An estimated 339 million people globally had asthma in 2016.

Asthma is a common disease in both children and adults. People living with asthma frequently have difficulty breathing and wheezing brought on by stress, exertion, and irritants in the air. Most mortality from asthma occurs in low- and middle-income countries. Usually, it has a low fatality rate compared to other chronic diseases.

However, in 2014, African-Americans were about three times more likely to die from asthma-related causes than the white population. Black children are over four times more likely to be admitted to hospital for asthma compared to white children. African-Americans do not only have a higher prevalence of asthma than whites; they are also plagued with higher rates of asthma-related morbidity and death. Multiple factors contribute to this disparity in prevalence rates including socioeconomic status, environmental factors and, plausibly, genetics.

Section 3: Policing Race

While it is well established that genetic factors strongly affect susceptibility to asthma, it is uncertain the extent to which genetic variations contribute to the disparity in asthma prevalence, morbidity and mortality in different races.

African-Americans living in low-income areas have a higher prevalence of asthma and are at a greater risk of asthma-related death. Evidence suggests that both the African-American race and lower socioeconomic status are independent risk factors for asthma prevalence, morbidity, and mortality and affect the rate of asthma diagnosis in African-Americans. Patients who lack sufficient financial support or health insurance are at greater risk of asthma-related mortality.

The quality of air breathed, which depends on the degree of environmental pollution, contributes to the asthma morbidity of urban residents in the United States like African-Americans. Obesity, which is now pandemic, is another risk factor for bronchial asthma. These are two issues that particularly plague the Black people of American inner cities.

Unfortunately, the American health care system has many inequalities that negatively impact people of color. These inequalities lead to gaps in health insurance coverage, poor access to health care with higher mortalities, poor health maintenance behavior due to lack of follow up, and poor provider-patient communication. The result is poorer outcomes for Black people living with asthma.

Police brutality is inordinately a cause of mortality amongst the people of color. In the United States, African-Americans disproportionately bear the brunt of these brutalities. Many of them, unfortunately, MAY have some underlying or undiagnosed health challenges like asthma. Incidents of police brutality involving all races tend to be targeted at lower-income people who often do not have the financial resources to effectively publicize their complaints of police brutality or to seek redress.

There are no large studies on the knowledge, attitudes and practices of police officers concerning asthma. It is uncertain that police officers are aware of the symptoms, signs and immediate care that can be given to asthmatic patients in custody until help arrives.

In 2014 there was a case of an asthmatic in police custody who kept saying he was asthmatic and could not breathe in Los Angeles. The police officers could not recognize the warning signs. That inmate died. If the officers knew how to recognize the clinical tale-tell signs, he might have been alive today.

The doctor who performed an autopsy on Eric Garner testified that a police officer choked him with enough force that it triggered a "lethal cascade" of events, ending in a fatal asthma attack. How many more Black men have died in the hands of the police because of their asthma? How many more must die before we make the needed changes?

There is a need to put an end to racism in the United States and the world at large. Given that asthma is prevalent in communities of color, the police must embrace better tactics in apprehending, restraining and keeping custody of suspects. We must de-emphasize the use of force and firearms while we work to improve the health and health care of all communities.

About the Authors

Obasi Okorie, MBBCh, FMCPaed, is a pediatric endocrinologist at King Abdulaziz Specialist Hospital in Saudi Arabia.

Ekemini Hogan is a pediatrician with the University of Uyo Teaching Hospital. She is also a fellow of the Nigerian National Postgraduate Medical College of Paediatrics.

Utibe Effiong, M.D., M.P.H., is a physician, public health scientist, and clinical assistant professor of medicine at Central Michigan University.

Section 4: Race, Education and Achievement

4.1 Teaching About Racism Is Essential for Education
   By the Editors of *Scientific American*
4.2 Where Are the Black Women in STEM Leadership?
   By Erika Jefferson
4.3 This Is What the Race Gap in Academia Looks Like
   By Amanda Montañez
4.4 The Brilliance Paradox: What Really Keeps Women and Minorities from Excelling in Academia
   By Andrei Cimpian and Sarah-Jane Leslie

Teaching About Racism Is Essential for Education

By the Editors of *Scientific American*

Elected officials who campaigned against critical race theory (CRT), the study of how social structures perpetuate racial inequality and injustice, are being sworn into office all over the U.S. These candidates captured voters' attention by vilifying CRT, which has become a catch-all to describe any teaching about racial injustice. Lessons about the genocide of Native Americans, slavery, segregation and systemic racism would harm children, these candidates argued. Calling its inclusion divisive, some states have enacted legislation banning CRT from school curricula altogether.

This regressive agenda threatens children's education by propagating a falsified view of reality in which American history and culture are outcomes of white virtue. It is part of a larger program of avoiding any truths that make some people uncomfortable, which sometimes allows in active disinformation, such as creationism. Children are especially susceptible to misinformation, as Melinda Wenner Moyer writes in "Schooled in Lies."

It is crucial for young people to learn about equity and social justice so they can thrive in our increasingly global, multilingual and multicultural society. When students become aware of the structural origins of inequality, they better understand the foundations of American society. They are also better equipped to comprehend, interpret and integrate into their worldviews the science they learn in their classrooms and experience in their lives.

Pondering racial, ethnic and socioeconomic disparities helps students understand, for example, why COVID death rates among Black, Latino and Native American people were much higher than those of white people as the pandemic began. They can better comprehend why people of color are far more likely to be subjected to the ravages of pollution and climate change or how a legacy of

Section 4: Race, Education and Achievement

U.S. science that experimented on Black and Indigenous Americans may have led to distrust of doctors and health care.

Removing conversations around race and society removes truth and reality from education. This political interference is nothing new—political and cultural ideologues have fought for years to remove subjects such as evolution, Earth history and sex education from classrooms and textbooks, despite the evidence that sex ed helps to prevent unwanted pregnancy and sexually transmitted diseases, that evolution explains all life on Earth and that the world is older than a few thousand years.

Many of the school districts that brought in anti-CRT board members are the same ones that refuse to mandate masks, despite the evidence that masks can prevent the spread of COVID. These school officials also rail against vaccine mandates as a violation of personal choice. It is the same prioritization of individuals over community and a discomfort with hard truths that characterize the movement against the teaching of true history.

Fortunately, efforts to limit children's education face stark opposition. The American Civil Liberties Union describes initiatives to quash discussions of racism in classrooms as "anathema to free speech." And the U.S. Department of Education is debating a series of American History and Civics standards that include introducing "racially, ethnically, culturally, and linguistically diverse perspectives into teaching and learning." Caught in the middle are teachers who are trying to educate children during a pandemic.

While many parents of school-aged children supported anti-CRT campaigns, voters with no connection to the classroom helped significantly to tip these elections. Parents and educators must bring the conversation back to teaching children about reality. EdAllies, a Minnesota-based educational-support nonprofit, is encouraging teachers to reach out to parents and administrators to explain the necessity of antiracist content in their lessons, as a way to build community support.

All over the U.S., school board meetings are being taken over by fear of the inclusion bogeyman. And after our recent elections, more board members have the power to act against lessons they dislike. Today, tomorrow and for as long as these elected officials are in office, it is the children and the teachers who will pay the price for an incomplete education. We must work toward a school experience that includes narratives of discrimination, social justice and inequality as truths we can learn from so that history might not repeat itself.

Where Are the Black Women in STEM Leadership?

By Erika Jefferson

Today, Black women are working in every industry imaginable and doing jobs that, just a generation or two ago, we could only dream of. Yet the number of those working at senior levels in STEM fields remains distressingly low. In March, the National Science Foundation reported that in 2016 alone, Black women earned more than 33,000 bachelor's degrees in science and engineering, and 24 percent of doctorates awarded to Black women were in STEM. But that same report showed that in 2017, only 5 percent of managerial jobs in STEM were held by Black women and men combined. So, where are we?

This disparity is occurring amid record employment levels, and there is a critical need for qualified technical workers—but we cannot expect women and underrepresented minorities to remain in work environments where they cannot grow and thrive. We also cannot expect girls to enter fields where they do not see positive role models. It is imperative that we stop the constant drip from the leaky STEM pipeline by working hard to retain women—and especially underrepresented women of color—from the middle to the end.

Not only is this important for today's workforce needs, but also for tomorrow's. Despite our best efforts to encourage future generations to become scientists and engineers, there is no guarantee they will enter or stay in the STEM workforce once their education is complete. Without an influx of new talent each year, the United States will fall further behind other nations in innovative and technological advances. Let's spend more time and money to ensure we can keep those Black women who are determined enough to make science a career.

At one time, Fortune 500 companies had their pick of the top graduates from the best schools, but no more. A brilliant young engineer from a top university will be heavily recruited but is just as likely to create her own company as go to work for a long-established one. Some industries are already feeling the impact of this and are trying to adapt. In the last several years, there have been some attempts to stem this rising tide by reaching out to a broader demographic of potential workers.

While leaders may say this is to address the ongoing gender imbalance in technical fields, dig a little deeper and it becomes clear companies already know they will not have enough capable talent to fill these roles in the digital revolution and are trying prepare for the loss of a preferred demographic.

Globally, we are still struggling to attract and retain women in STEM fields. While the problem has been getting more attention, the change is occurring much too slowly. The underlying reasons why diversity and inclusivity have not taken root have not changed over time. Women and minorities cite feelings of isolation, mistreatment by colleagues and management, and lack of opportunities for advancement as the reasons they leave STEM fields.

One solution is to create more diversity and inclusivity in emerging technologies by preparing underrepresented women already in STEM for roles in leadership. These efforts would provide the skills necessary for diverse women with traditional STEM degrees to rapidly transition into emerging technologies such as artificial intelligence, virtual reality, the Internet of Things and cybersecurity, while leveraging their previous experience and preparing them for leadership. Such resources could ensure women with technical backgrounds get the support necessary to become leaders in these industries far more quickly than we could by waiting on the next generation of workers to advance.

And more diverse leaders in these fields are needed for there to be a significant impact that creates the enduring change of including women and people of color in all areas of technology. It is critically important girls and women around the world have role models, mentors and champions in the workplace of the future who look like them. By training diverse women already in technical roles to become leaders, the entire ecosystem benefits. Women scientists and engineers understand the challenges of working in male-dominated fields and can better prepare others wanting to learn how to excel in management and entrepreneurship.

In 2015, we launched Black Women in Science and Engineering (BWISE) to support underrepresented women via networking, mentoring and career development. The group consists of women with degrees in science, technology, engineering and math, even if they no longer work in these areas. Research has shown diverse companies are more productive and successful. A dire shortage of STEM workers is predicted in the next 20 years, so it is imperative that young Black women be included in the workforce. Few companies have workforce affinity groups (associations based on shared experiences and backgrounds); these types of organizations are known to build support and morale among workers who feel acknowledged, valued and included within the larger corporate structure.

With BWISE, employees can get what they need despite—or in addition to—company offerings. Here, they have a safe space to discuss challenges and receive coaching, training and insight outside of the workplace. Companies can sponsor employees to be a part of BWISE to supplement their existing diversity efforts and can also assist by bringing in speakers and supporting our events. The organization helps to prepare, train and develop the next generation of Black women leaders in STEM.

We also have hosted successful networking events across the country in Atlanta, Austin, Chicago, Houston and Washington. Each event attracts the best and brightest in the STEM field, ranging from mid-career to top-level executives. In 2019, we will expand to three more cities—Boston, Dallas and New York—and provide more in-depth trainings in emerging technologies to meet the career demands of our membership.

The network of BWISE chapters and women around the world consists of experts and thought leaders in business, government and academia who are focused on engaging and empowering girls and women everywhere to join the digital revolution. Our members from the U.S., Europe and Africa are poised to become leaders in their own countries, impacting the lives of underrepresented people around the globe. By creating a more diverse workforce globally in emerging technology fields, we can help reduce gender-based financial inequities and be better prepared for the workplace of the future.

About the Author

Erika Jefferson is the president and founder of Black Women in Science and Engineering (BWISE), an organization focused on bridging the leadership gap for Black women in STEM. She received her MBA from Georgia Tech and her BS in chemical engineering from LSU. She has worked for top companies such as Amoco, BP, Chevron and Praxair in a myriad of leadership roles ranging from sales/business development to supply chain and operations excellence.

This Is What the Race Gap in Academia Looks Like

By Amanda Montañez

In a *Scientific American* article published in September 2017 (see page 99), scientists Sarah-Jane Leslie and Andrei Cimpian described how certain fields of study—such as philosophy, for example—seem to ascribe an outsized value to brilliance, a trait generally considered innate rather than learned, among its scholars. Whereas on its face this attitude seems relatively innocuous, Leslie and Cimpian observed that it tends to coincide with a marked lack of diversity in the academic disciplines in which it prevails. They wrote:

> Philosophers seek a certain quality of mind—regardless of whose mind it is. This seemingly logical preference quickly becomes problematic, however, in light of certain shared societal notions that incorrectly associate superior intellect with some groups—for example, white males—more than others.

To test their hypothesis that the "brilliance" factor might have a negative impact on diversity, the two researchers conducted a survey of nearly 2,000 academic professionals, measuring the emphasis on natural genius within each of 30 fields. They combined their results with data from the National Science Foundation on the races and genders of those earning PhDs in the same disciplines.

The data set that emerged included remarkable findings about both gender and racial imbalances in academia. But as the article focused heavily on gender, and as these demographics involve different population-wide baselines, I thought the subset of data on African-American PhDs deserved its own visualization.

In the midst of Black History Month, these data serve as a not-so-subtle reminder the legacy of racism and inequality in the U.S. persists. And academia—like all institutions sorely lacking in racial and ethnic diversity—is the poorer for it. The work of Leslie

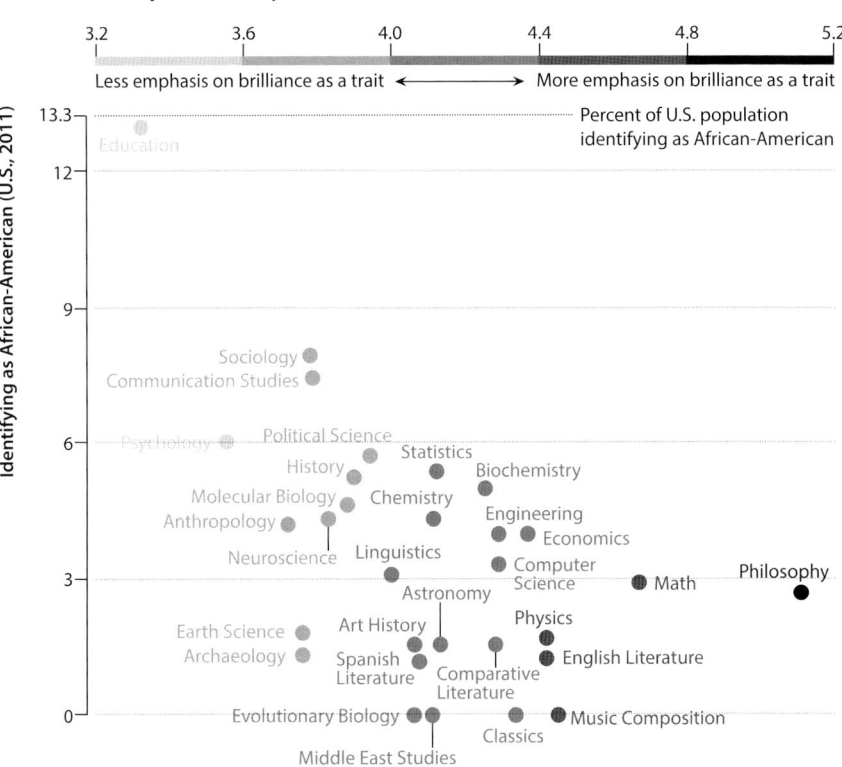

Credit: Amanda Montañez

Source: "Expectations of Brilliance Underlie Gender Distributions Across Academic Disciplines," by Sarah-Jane Leslie et al., in *Science*, Vol. 347; January 16, 2015 (PhD data); U.S. Census Bureau (population data)

and Cimpian represent at least the foundation of a step forward. However, as they soberly acknowledge, "The hard work of figuring out how best to put all this information to use—how to intervene—lies ahead of us."

About the Author

Amanda Montañez is an associate graphics editor at Scientific American.

The Brilliance Paradox: What Really Keeps Women and Minorities from Excelling in Academia

By Andrei Cimpian and Sarah-Jane Leslie

In the 1980s philosophers would sometimes speak of "the beam"—a metaphorical spotlight of intellectual brilliance that could illuminate even the most complex philosophical conundrums. Only some lucky philosophers were ever born with the Beam, and their work represented the gold standard of the field. Anyone who lacked the Beam was forever condemned to trail behind them intellectually.

One of us (Leslie) would share this sort of story whenever we would see each other at conferences. The two of us were trained in different disciplines (Leslie in philosophy and Cimpian in psychology), but we studied similar topics, so we would get together regularly to catch up on research and talk about our experiences as members of our respective fields. Psychology and philosophy are quite similar in their substance (in fact, psychology was a branch of philosophy until the mid-1800s), but the stories we told painted a picture of two fields with vastly different views on what is important for success. Much more so than psychologists, philosophers value a certain kind of person— the brilliant superstar with an exceptional mind. Psychologists, in contrast, are relatively more likely to believe that the leading lights in their field grew to achieve their positions through hard work and experience.

At first, we viewed philosophy's obsession with brilliance as a quirk—a little strange but innocuous. Other things seemed to present bigger problems in Leslie's field, such as its inability to attract women and minorities. Despite sustained attention to issues of underrepresentation in recent years and some efforts to alleviate them, women still accounted for fewer than 30 percent of the doctoral degrees granted in philosophy in 2015, and Black people made up only 1 percent of philosophy Ph.D.s. The field of psychology, in contrast, has been quite successful in attracting and retaining women (72 percent of newly minted Ph.D.s), and Black people held 6 percent of its 2015 doctoral degrees. Admittedly, these figures still fall short of their share of the general population, but they are nonetheless six times the ratio in philosophy.

We could not wrap our minds around the discrepancy. Our fields have so much in common—both philosophers and psychologists ask questions about how people perceive and understand the world, how they decide between right and wrong, how they learn and use language, and so on. Even the few salient differences—such as psychologists' greater use of statistics and randomized experiments—are becoming blurred nowadays with the huge increase in the popularity of experimental philosophy, in which philosophers conduct surveys and experiments to explore different perspectives on morality, for example. How could two such closely related fields be so vastly different in membership?

A Brilliant Idea

The closest thing either of us has ever had to a eureka moment came several years ago when we connected two threads running through the anecdotes we had been sharing. We were having dinner with a group of philosophers and psychologists at a conference, and the conversation happened to turn, in quick succession, from philosophers' infatuation with brilliance to the gender gap in their field. This chance juxtaposition brought to mind for us a connection we had never considered before: maybe the premium that philosophers place on brilliance is actually the reason so few of their colleagues are women or minorities. We did not discount the benefits of brilliance. Rather we wondered whether genius was more easily overlooked in women and Black people. Could it be that insistence on the need for a keen intellect in a particular field was tantamount to hanging a "Keep Out" sign to discourage any newcomers who did not resemble that field's current members?

On the surface, an emphasis on brilliance does not favor one group over another; cognitive ability is not intrinsically tied to gender or race. Philosophers seek a certain quality of mind—regardless of whose mind it is. This seemingly logical preference quickly becomes problematic, however, in light of certain shared societal notions that incorrectly associate superior intellect with some groups—for example, white males—more than others.

Even among the academics present that night, one of the views expressed was that men and women just thought differently. Women were alleged to be more practical and anchored in reality, whereas men were more willing to engage in the kind of counterfactual, abstract reasoning that is viewed as a sign of philosophical brilliance. We started to wonder whether such stereotypes, which amount to equating brilliance with men, might well dissuade women from entering a field that holds this quality in high esteem. Moreover, current members of such a field might themselves hold different expectations about the prospects of men and women and might evaluate and encourage them differently as a result. The same logic extends to race: our country has a long history of portraying Black people as intellectually inferior, which is particularly likely to affect their participation in a field that focuses so single-mindedly on the quality of one's intellect. Considering these stereotyped attitudes, which are unsupported by science, philosophy's fascination with brilliance may have a real impact on its diversity.

Later that night the two of us talked about our insight. We speculated about whether its implications extend beyond our home disciplines. Talk of brilliance is common in academia and—it seemed to us—quite common in fields that have similar issues with diversity, such as science, technology, engineering and mathematics. Might our anecdotal comparison of philosophy and psychology have something new to say about the underrepresentation of women and minorities in these disciplines?

The more we thought about it, the more we realized that our brilliance hypothesis might also explain some of the variability in gender and race gaps *among* different scientific fields. For example, women make up nearly 50 percent of doctoral degrees in biochemistry but just slightly more than 30 percent of Ph.D.s in organic chemistry. The difference cannot easily be explained by the content of the fields, in which there is considerable overlap, or by their history—biochemistry emerged from organic chemistry at about the same time psychology separated out of philosophy as an independent discipline. We wondered whether the demographic differences between such sibling subjects, as well as more generally among scientific fields, could be explained in part by the extent to which they emphasize exceptional intellectual talent as the key to success.

Successful Mindsets

Our early conjectures quickly reminded us of the rich body of work developed by psychologist Carol S. Dweck of Stanford University. Dweck and her colleagues have shown that one's beliefs about ability matter greatly for one's ultimate success. A person who sees talent as a stable trait (a "fixed mindset" in Dweck's terminology) is motivated to show off this aptitude and avoid mistakes, which presumably reflect the limits of that gift. In contrast, a person who adopts a "growth mindset" sees his or her current capacity as a work in progress. In other words, ability is a malleable quantity that can usually be increased with more effort and better strategies. For a person with a growth mindset, mistakes are not an indictment but rather a valuable signal highlighting which of their skills are in need of work.

Although Dweck initially studied mindsets in individuals, she and Mary Murphy, now at Indiana University Bloomington, recently suggested that organized groups of people, such as companies

Section 4: Race, Education and Achievement

and clubs, may also hold these sorts of views. We took that idea a step further and considered whether they might permeate entire disciplines as well. The fascination with brilliance in philosophy and other areas could conceivably create an atmosphere in which displays of intellectual prowess are rewarded and imperfections are to be avoided at all costs. In combination with the stereotypes suggesting that genius is unevenly distributed across groups, such a field-wide perspective could easily turn toxic for members of stereotyped groups, such as women or Black people. After all, it is easy to "see" imperfections and inadequacies in those people whom you expect to have them.

Several long phone conversations later, we had a tentative plan for putting our ideas to the test. We would contact academic professionals from across a wide range of disciplines and ask them whether they thought that some form of exceptional intellectual talent was necessary for success in their field. We would then look up statistics on the gender and racial/ethnic composition of the people obtaining Ph.D.s in these disciplines, which the National Science Foundation freely supplies on its Web site. If our hunch was correct, we should see that those disciplines that place more value on brilliance would tend to have fewer female and Black Ph.D.s. This pattern should hold not just at the macro level—when comparing the hard sciences, for example, with the social sciences and the humanities—but also *within* these broad domains for disciplines as similar as philosophy and psychology.

More than a year and thousands of e-mailed surveys later, we and our collaborators Meredith Meyer of Otterbein University in Ohio and Edward Freeland of Princeton University finally had an answer to some of our questions. Equal parts relieved and exhilarated, we saw that the answers received from almost 2,000 academics across 30 fields matched the distribution of Ph.D.s in the way we had expected. Fields that placed more value on brilliance also conferred fewer Ph.D.s on women and Black candidates. The greater the emphasis on this single fixed trait, the fewer doctoral degrees were awarded to either of these groups. The proportion of female and

Black Ph.D.s in psychology, for example, was higher than the parallel proportions for philosophy, math or physics.

Next, we separated the responses in the physical and biological sciences from those in the humanities and social sciences. Analyses of these subgroups indicated that a stronger emphasis on brilliance correlated with fewer female and Black Ph.D.s regardless of whether we compared physics with biology or philosophy with sociology. It seemed that we had stumbled onto an explanation that was general enough to describe the representation of multiple stereotyped groups in fields across the entire academic spectrum.

Alternative Ideas

Our excitement about these data aside, all we had really shown at this point was a correlation between the presumed desirability of a fixed trait—brilliance—and a dearth of women or Black people in a given field. We had not yet demonstrated cause and effect. Certainly many other plausible explanations for the gender imbalances have been proffered over the years—from a heavier workload that favored single men and those with wives who did not work outside the home to a supposed female preference for working with living organisms, as opposed to inanimate objects. We needed to determine whether we were bringing something new to the table—perhaps our explanation reduced to one that had been previously offered.

We carefully examined the most common alternatives. For instance, did our brilliance measure simply track differences between fields in their reliance on math? We looked at the math portion of incoming students' Graduate Record Examinations (GREs) as a proxy. Beliefs about brilliance still predicted women's representation above and beyond those scores. Similarly, we found no support for the common view that women are underrepresented in "high-powered fields" because they prefer a better work-family balance. We asked the academics in our sample how many hours they worked per week—both on- and off-campus. Taking into account these differences in workload did not, however, reduce the explanatory power of beliefs about brilliance; this single variable still predicted the magnitude of gender gaps across the 30 disciplines. We also considered the prevalent thought that women might be more interested in working with (and have a better intuitive understanding of) people, whereas men prefer inanimate systems. But an analysis of the many branches of philosophy, for example, that do in fact consider people—and are still dominated by men—basically blew that idea out of contention.

As often happens in research, this initial study made it clear to us how much we did *not* yet know about the phenomenon that we were investigating. For example, we realized it would be important to know if academics' beliefs about brilliance predict gender and race gaps at earlier points in students' educational trajectories. We were very interested in testing our idea at the bachelor's level, which is the gateway to students' later careers. Do field-level messages about the importance of brilliance relate to the majors that young women and Black students ultimately pursue?

The answer to this question is yes, as we reported in *PLOS ONE* in 2016 when we analyzed anonymous student evaluations of their college instructors on RateMyProfessors.com. We found that undergraduates were nearly twice as likely to describe male professors as "brilliant" or a "genius" compared with female professors. In contrast, they used such terms as "excellent" or "amazing" equally often for men and women on the popular Web site. We determined that the overall amount of talk about brilliance and genius in the student reviews (which is a proxy for a field's emphasis on these qualities) correlated closely with a lack of diversity in completed majors.

Origins of Stereotypes

Further investigation showed that nonacademics share similar notions of which fields require brilliance. Exposure to these ideas at home or school could discourage young members of stereotyped groups from pursuing certain careers (such as those in science or engineering) before they even set foot on a college campus.

At this point, we realized we needed to investigate the acquisition of these stereotypes. When do young people in our culture start thinking that some groups have more brilliant people in them? On the one hand, it could be that this stereotype emerges late in development, after sustained exposure to relevant cultural input (for example, media portrayals of brilliance and gender-biased expectations from parents, teachers, professors and peers). On the other hand, evidence from developmental psychology suggests that children are cultural sponges—incredibly sensitive to signals in their social environments. In fact, youngsters in the early elementary grades seem to have already absorbed the stereotypes that associate math with boys and reading with girls. From this perspective, we might expect that stereotypes about brilliance would also be acquired early in life.

To explore this idea, we asked hundreds of five-, six- and seven-year-old boys and girls many questions that measured whether they associated being "really, really smart" (our child-friendly translation of "brilliant") with their gender. The results, which we published in 2017 in *Science*, were consistent with the literature on the early acquisition of gender stereotypes yet were still shocking to us. Male and female five-year-olds showed no difference in their self-assessment. But by age six, girls were less likely than boys to think that members of their gender are "really, really smart."

Finding these stereotypes so early in childhood made us ask whether they might already begin to constrain boys' and girls' interests. We introduced another group of five-, six- and seven-year-olds to unfamiliar gamelike activities that we described as being "for children who are really, really smart." We then compared boys' and girls' interest in these activities at each age. The results revealed no gender differences at age five but significantly greater interest from boys at six and seven years of age—which is exactly where we saw the stereotypes emerge. In addition, the children's own stereotypes directly predicted their interest in these novel activities. The more a child associated brilliance with the opposite gender, the less interested he or she was in playing our games for "really, really smart children." This evidence suggests an early link between stereotypes about brilliance and children's aspirations. Over the rest of childhood development, this link may funnel many capable girls away from disciplines that our society perceives as being primarily for brilliant people.

The hard work of figuring out how best to put all this information to use—how to intervene—lies ahead of us. But a few suggestions follow pretty directly from the evidence we have so far. Minimizing talk of genius or brilliance with students and protégés may be a relatively easy and effective way of making one's field more welcoming for members of groups that are negatively stereotyped in this respect. Given current societal stereotypes, messages that portray this trait as singularly necessary may needlessly discourage talented members of stereotyped groups. The changes may need to go a little deeper than talk, however, and tackle some of the entrenched, systemic issues that accompany a field's fascination with brilliance. Refraining from mentioning the Beam will not help young women in philosophy if the rest of the field's practices continue to be implicitly anchored in the idea that brilliance is all that matters.

Another key takeaway is that we may need to intervene earlier than conventional wisdom suggests. Our developmental data indicate that some of the psychological processes that work against diversity in fields that value brilliance can be traced all the way back to elementary school. Waiting until college to step in and ensure that all young people have a fair shot at finding the careers that might suit them no longer seems like the best-timed intervention—we as a society would be wise to encourage a growth perspective, as opposed to a fixed-trait mindset, in young children as well.

About the Authors

Andrei Cimpian is a professor of psychology at New York University.

Sarah-Jane Leslie is the Class of 1943 Professor of Philosophy at Princeton University.

Section 5: Racism in Science and Technology

5.1 Silence Is Never Neutral; Neither Is Science
By 500 Women Scientists Leadership

5.2 How to Study Racial Disparities
By Bryan Schonfeld and Sam Winter-Levy

5.3 Black Images Matter: How Cameras Helped, and Sometimes Harmed, Black People
By Ainissa G. Ramirez

5.4 The Racist Legacy of Computer-Generated Humans
By Theodore Kim

Silence Is Never Neutral; Neither Is Science

By 500 Women Scientists Leadership

Disclaimer: We are publishing this piece as 500 Women Scientists Leadership to protect the authors, members of 500 Women Scientists, from the career repercussions of authoring an anti-racism piece. That in itself speaks to the very issues we highlight in this article.

Amidst #BlackLivesMatter protests and resounding calls for justice, many scientists, academic institutions and science organizations remain eerily silent. While the coronavirus pandemic highlighted the importance of science and evidence, the #ScienceNotSilence sentiments seem to stop short of extending to another major threat to people in the U.S. and across the world—systemic racism and race-based violence.

Racism has permeated this country since its inception, leading to a health crisis in Black and brown communities. Look no further than the impacts of COVID-19: in the United States, Black populations experience disproportionately more coronavirus diagnoses and deaths. Amid loud (and justifiable!) calls to protect and elevate the role of science, too many scientists and scientific organizations are eerily silent on the issues of racism and social justice—issues that are embedded into the history and practice of science.

Why does this matter? Because as every scientist knows, ignoring facts doesn't make them go away. Scientists live in societies and both internalize and reflect broader societal norms, just like everyone else. Every one of us brings different lived experiences, worldviews and implicit and explicit biases to our work. Because science is still dominated by largely white and male perspectives, many scientists have the privilege to look away from discrimination and racism or avoid having to engage in conflict around these topics. Too many

Section 5: Racism in Science and Technology

scientists today continue to downplay or outright erase the role science has played in perpetuating anti-Black racism and violence.

Scientific "progress" is built on racism in many cases. Ronald Fisher, a pioneer of statistics, is also a pioneer of eugenics. The HeLa cells that are so widely used in laboratories across the United States were stolen from Henrietta Lacks without her consent. The field of gynecology was born of experiments done on enslaved women and children. Scientists and public health officials withheld treatment from hundreds of Black men in Alabama who had syphilis, in the now infamous Tuskeegee Experiment, just to watch what would happen as this devastating disease progressed. The fact that the NIH does not even acknowledge the problematic history of the HeLa cells on its Web pages dedicated to Henrietta Lacks' legacy perfectly illustrates the refusal of science to grapple with its racist history.

Ignoring science's legacy of racism or a wider culture shaped by white supremacy doesn't make scientists "objective." It makes them complicit.

If one of the objectives of science is to serve society, then scientists must ask themselves: Which parts of society are we serving? And who is the "we" to begin with?

Scientists love evidence. And the data show a clear problem: in 2016 only 9 percent and 13.5 percent of science bachelor's degrees were awarded to African Americans and Latinos respectively. In that same year, only 5 percent of recipients of doctoral degrees in science and engineering were women from underrepresented minorities (Black or African American, Hispanic or Latino, and American Indian or Alaska Native), and men from those populations accounted for a mere 3.8 percent. Today in the U.S., almost 70 percent of scientists and engineers employed full time are white. For this majority, racial harassment, discrimination and state sanctioned violence are abstract concepts, not everyday worries. And this perpetuates a cycle: scientists of color are unrepresented, unsupported, harassed, discredited, ignored, or pushed out. This is not only morally wrong and profoundly unfair; it's also devastating to science itself.

Let's be clear: scientific institutions must immediately get to work on rooting out anti-Black racism and all forms of racism and discrimination. The pervasive silence on racism across science institutions is self-reinforcing; it creates a culture where talking about racism is actively discouraged and where Black, Latino/a and Indigenous scientists cannot bring their whole selves to their work. It also means science may not even be asking the right questions in the first place.

For example, the evidence is clear that climate change will disproportionately affect marginalized populations, a pattern that we have seen brutally demonstrated by the COVID-19 pandemic. And yet, the communities of epidemiologists, virologists and climate scientists tasked with studying these issues or shaping and implementing policies around them are profoundly unrepresentative of those populations. The people most affected and most familiar with the underlying issues are not driving the research agenda.

If we want science to help tackle our biggest challenges—from global pandemics to climate change—science institutions must train, hire and retain Black, Latino/a and Indigenous scholars. As it stands, not only are non-white scientists leaving science, but those who remain face hostile working environments and productivity sapped by the constant trauma of the news cycle. While the uptick in DEI efforts across academic institutions and science organizations is commendable, diversity, equity and inclusion (DEI) efforts that do not actively address the root causes of the trauma will always fall short.

If scientists don't explicitly say #BlackLivesMatter, if they don't speak up on justice and social issues, they risk overlooking solutions, discarding talent, and perpetuating toxic power dynamics. We must all hold ourselves and each other accountable to dismantle the systems of oppression that persist in our society, the very systems that claimed the lives of George Floyd and countless other Black people. That work should start by denouncing racial injustice and violence in no uncertain terms, but it cannot end there.

What can scientists, academic institutions, and scientific organizations do?

- Create robust strategies to dismantle systemic racism within your institutions.
- Train, hire and support scientists of color.
- Hire external antiracism educators to help staff and trainees implement new practices.
- Require all employees and trainees to take bystander intervention training, which has been shown to be most effective in effecting true cultural change.
- Hire independent DEI consultants to assess organizational culture.
- Design and implement a reward system for mentorship and outreach, as these responsibilities often fall disproportionately on underrepresented members of the faculty.
- Require security staff to obtain regular antiracist de-escalation training.
- Break contracts with local police, and pledge not to call the police for nonviolent offenses.

The work of dismantling institutional racism must start at home, in our scientific institutions. Addressing racism in science has to include fundamentally changing the scientific institutions themselves, anything short of that is just lip service.

Silence is never neutral. Neither is science.

How to Study Racial Disparities
By Bryan Schonfeld and Sam Winter-Levy

As the United States grapples with the national reckoning over race prompted by the killing of George Floyd, it has become increasingly clear that even a pandemic does not strike equally. Nationwide, Black people have been 3.7 times as likely as white people to die of COVID-19, taking age into account; in some states, Black people have died of COVID-19 at age-adjusted rates five to nine times higher than those of white people.

Against this backdrop, the importance of studying racial disparities in social, economic, and public health outcomes has rarely been clearer. But researchers, and the journalists who report on their findings, should exercise caution in trying to uncover the *sources* of these stark discrepancies. Studying race, and in particular the relationship between race and social outcomes like health or police violence, comes with both statistical and conceptual challenges, which make understanding exactly why Black people are dying from COVID-19 at higher rates harder than it might seem.

Perhaps the biggest issue arises out of what statisticians call "post-treatment bias." Because racial identity is assigned at birth, it affects a wide range of other aspects of people's lives—where someone lives, how they're educated, the sorts of opportunities they have, and how much money they earn. To understand the effect of race on a certain outcome—say, police violence, or the likelihood of death among COVID-19 patients—scholars will often control for factors like education, income, health status or occupation. But all these variables are "post-treatment," or downstream, of race, in the sense that race itself can shape how a person is raised, educated and employed. Controlling for these variables can distort any results that scholars may find.

Consider the following analogy: if researchers set out to investigate whether smoking leads to death, but controlled for whether someone gets lung cancer, they might find that smoking doesn't increase mortality—because they've effectively removed an important pathway by which smoking influences health. What's more, by controlling for lung cancer, they're now comparing the life spans of smokers who don't get lung cancer, who are likely to be unusually healthy, to nonsmokers without lung cancer (and comparing nonsmokers who get lung cancer, a highly unusual group, to smokers who get lung cancer). In the context of race, controlling for almost any socioeconomic or health variable—as most studies on ethnic disparities in COVID-19 deaths do—can create serious biases in an analysis, calling many empirical results into question.

Similar issues abound in the study of race and policing. Take the recent debate over whether there is evidence of racism in American policing. Roland Fryer, an economist at Harvard, found that police shoot white, Black and Hispanic Americans whom they've stopped at equal rates. However, as political scientists Dean Knox, Will Lowe, and Jonathan Mummolo point out, if there is initial discrimination in who gets stopped in the first place, estimating racial disparities in how people are treated once they've been stopped becomes much more complicated—especially since police officers are more likely to stop Black and Hispanic people than white people, and more of those stops are unjustified. If Black people are stopped by police for lesser (or nonexistent) offenses, "equal treatment" in terms of the use of force would actually indicate deeply unequal policing overall. Being stopped by the police is "post-treatment" to race, and failing to account for this bias can lead to erroneous conclusions that may mask the extent of racism in American institutions.

A second challenge, as the political scientists Maya Sen and Omar Wasow point out, comes from the instability of racial labels. As one study concluded, "No two measures of race will capture the same information." In one 19-year survey of thousands of Americans, a full 20 percent of the sample changed either how they were racially classified by others or how they identified themselves. Survey respondents even changed identification in response to life events: incarceration, unemployment or having an income below the poverty line made respondents more likely to identify as Black, while people who get married are more likely to be seen as and identify as white.

Between the 2000 and 2010 censuses, nearly 10 million respondents altered their self-identified race or response regarding Hispanic origin; only 41 percent of Hispanics identified their race and ethnic origin the same way in both censuses. Another study found that homicide victims were more likely to be classified as Black on their death certificates, while people who died of cirrhosis of the liver were more likely to be classified as Native American—even accounting for the race of the victim as given by their next of kin.

Throughout American history, racial boundaries have shifted considerably. Chinese Americans in the Mississippi Delta were once classified as almost Black, while a 1974 U.S. federal committee on racial and ethnic definitions struggled with how to categorize people of South Asian origin: it initially recommended they be labeled white/Caucasian before classifying them as Asian or Pacific Islanders.

And there are big differences in racial definitions across countries: in the United States, thanks to the so-called one-drop rule, a person with any Black heritage has historically been categorized as Black; in Brazil, an individual is not "Black" if he or she has any European ancestry.

In other words, racial identities are largely not biologically determined, but are instead the product of social forces. Yet as sociologist Ann Morning has documented, the biological view of race still dominates in biology textbooks and among biology undergraduates and biology professors in the U.S.. And when quantitative social scientists study race, they often just include a binary variable for Black or white in an equation. When this sort of research finds racial disparities in outcomes like COVID-19 mortality rates or police killings, it often raises more questions than it provides answers: it doesn't explain why or how race affects life outcomes, nor does it shed much light on potential policy interventions that could help.

But there are better ways to study race. In a 2016 paper, Sen and Wasow propose that researchers should think about race not as an essential set of unchangeable biological characteristics but rather as what they call "a bundle of sticks" that includes factors like skin color, dialect, neighborhood, genes, class, names, and region of ancestry. While "race" itself cannot be manipulated in a study, many of these traits, which are closely linked with what we mean by race, can be. By focusing only on one stick in the bundle at a time—rather than on the combination of ancestry, neighborhood, socioeconomic status, skin color, names, and the like that would be conveyed by a simple "race" variable—researchers can attempt to isolate exactly which factors lie behind the racial disparities we observe.

For example, researchers can manipulate the name on a resume to study how the perceived race of a job applicant affects their likelihood of getting hired. The late Harvard sociologist Devah Pager, for example, found that employers responded as much to an applicant with a stereotypically white name and a criminal record as they did to a Black applicant without one. Or researchers can try to isolate the role of perceived skin color, another stick in the bundle, in racial disparities in policing. In one recent paper in *Nature Human Behaviour*, which examines police stops around 7 P.M., researchers found that Black drivers were more likely to be stopped when it is sunnier; after sunset, a "veil of darkness" protects Black drivers from being racially profiled. Again, by focusing on one factor in the bundle of sticks—perceived skin color, in this case—the researchers isolated other factors that could drive disparities in traffic stops, such as socioeconomic and neighborhood characteristics.

Another way to avoid issues of post-treatment bias and the instability of racial labels is to focus on differences *within* a racial group, rather than attempting comparisons between them, to see which mechanisms might be driving differences in outcomes. To study educational disparities between Blacks and whites, for example, instead of simply conducting an analysis of educational outcomes across the population at large and controlling for race and socioeconomic factors—a common approach that is both contaminated by post-treatment bias and conceptually unclear—researchers could try to isolate within-group variation in one of the bundle of sticks plausibly related to education.

Take the Moving to Opportunity experiment, for example, which involved the random assignment of housing vouchers. Researchers have analyzed this experiment to compare the academic performance of Black youngsters from high-poverty neighborhoods to similarly situated Black youngsters in moderate-poverty neighborhoods, finding that neighborhoods can substantially influence socioeconomic outcomes.

Some of the pitfalls of across-group analysis can be seen in Charles Murray's notorious and deeply flawed book *The Bell Curve*, which asserted that white Americans possessed a genetic advantage in cognitive ability over Black Americans. Murray simply compared Black and white differences in IQ tests and concluded that these differences must be, at least in part, genetic. This analysis views race almost exclusively as an essential biological category, fails to address the complex mix of social factors underpinning racial identity, and is vulnerable to all the statistical biases discussed above. A more sophisticated research design examined Black individuals who varied in levels of European ancestry but shared a similar social environment and identity, and found no relationship between genes associated with white ancestry and cognitive ability. "By identifying meaningful within-group differences," Sen and Wasow commented, "scholars can narrow the causal mechanisms that explain disparate across-race outcomes."

In the context of COVID-19, researchers should avoid drawing too many conclusions about the underlying causes of racial disparities from studies that simply include a binary variable for race—whose "effect" is conceptually unclear—and that control for socioeconomic characteristics and health conditions that are likely downstream of race. A more promising approach would involve isolating one possible explanation for this gap—say, differences in neighborhood health institutions, incarceration rates, or particular occupational roles and health conditions—and studying differences within racial groups to gain insight into which factors might be driving racial disparities in COVID-19 mortality.

To create a more just society, we must understand the underlying causes of racial disparities in social, economic and public health outcomes. But while studying the extent of disparities between groups—such as the Black-white wealth gap or disparities in COVID-19 death rates—is essential, if researchers wish to explain the *causes* of these disparities they need to make sure they remain sensitive to the statistical, conceptual and historical complexities associated with race. Researchers are likely to make more progress if they approach race as a composite measure of linked characteristics like dialect, ancestry, neighborhood, class and skin color—rather than as a fixed biological category.

About the Authors

Bryan Schonfeld is a Ph.D. candidate in political science at Princeton University.

Sam Winter-Levy is a Ph.D. candidate in political science at Princeton University.

Black Images Matter: How Cameras Helped, and Sometimes Harmed, Black People

By Ainissa G. Ramirez

In the 19th century, the most photographed man in the world wasn't Walt Whitman or Ulysses S. Grant or even Abraham Lincoln. It was Frederick Douglass. The famous orator and abolitionist was known for using his eloquent voice to impart the horrors of slavery, which he had experienced firsthand. He traveled all over the country, speaking to large crowds and making arguments to end the enslavement of Black people. On the days when there were no scheduled lectures, he would visit a daguerreotype studio to have his picture taken. He enlisted these images as another thrust of his campaign, offering the public a positive view of a Black person to oppose the negative caricatures that were commonplace in newspapers. His handsome portrait was a weapon against these malicious images, because his photographs were sold by, and distributed from, the studios he visited. With them, picture by picture, he slowly changed the public's perception of an African-American. Frederick Douglass knew back in the 19th century that Black images mattered.

When Douglass had his pictures taken, rendering an image of a person was a democratic expression. For a small sum, the kitchen chemistry to sensitize a glass plate made it easy for anyone to have his or her image captured. Doing so became even easier as photography was adopted as an American pastime, and camera manufacturers not only produced film, but processed it. Taking pictures became a big business. And W.E.B. DuBois, an African-American scholar born about 50 years after Douglass, also had great hopes that it would serve the cause of racial justice. DuBois knew the power of displaying Black images to sway the American consciousness. And he used pictures to showcase his race's achievements with material that included portraits of educated Black individuals, images he showed in his Exhibit of American Negroes at the 1900 World's Fair in Paris.

But unlike Douglass, DuBois grew leery of photography. Although it was a powerful way to push back against the stereotypes, this tool was starting to work against him. DuBois noticed that "the average white photographer does not know how to deal with colored skins," he said. And the resulting pictures of Black people were often a "horrible botch."

In 1915, as DuBois struggled with images of Black people, photography—and portrayals of African-Americans in particular—took a hideous turn. That year D. W. Griffith released his film *The Birth of a Nation*. This movie fabricated a false narrative of the Civil War and offered a redemptive account of the acts of the Ku Klux Klan: Griffith depicted the white supremacist secret society saving the nation from lecherous Black people (who were actually white actors in blackface). His film became the most loved movie in the nation. It was even watched in the White House by its fan in chief, President Woodrow Wilson. Griffith was a masterful moviemaker who pioneered the close-up, scenic long shot, and the crosscut. And he created a film that further contaminated the country. Griffith, like DuBois and Douglass, knew the power of pictures.

Negative portrayals of Black Americans took on a new force as, within a year after *The Birth of a Nation*, the Great Migration from the South to the North began. While many books will say that African-Americans came to the North for jobs, a truer reason was that they were fleeing for their lives. Terror was the law of the land, and lynchings were very common. For many of these murders, cameras were ringside, capturing burned and broken Black bodies. These photographs were often sold and distributed. Unlike Douglass's portraits, they were not rendered to make African-Americans more human but less.

In this time, the U.S. was a hotbed of intimidation. As the number of lynchings increased, many spoke up against them, but their voices were largely ignored. The Herculean efforts of Black journalist Ida B. Wells, starting in the 1890s, brought these atrocities to the national attention. While Black people knew of them, what the mainstream world needed was proof. And Wells collected statistics of their occurrences and wrote up depictions of lynchings in her newspaper. Beginning in 1916, the NAACP picked up this work. It also found other means to make such murders a part of the public conversation: in the 1920s and 1930s, it flew a flag outside of its building stating, "A Man Was Lynched Yesterday." Wells and the NAACP used technology to provide hard evidence, and they filled the national consciousness with images and newspaper articles and flagpole alerts in an effort to create change.

The flash point for that change came from a picture. Lynchings had long been an exertion of power by whites. Then a Black mother named Mamie Till redirected the use of photography as an attack, wielding it against the attackers. She did so by allowing photographs of the open casket of her lynched son, Emmett Till. It was the picture of his mangled and bloated 14-year-old body that catalyzed the civil rights movement. Other pictures, of a Black woman arrested for refusing to give up her seat on a bus in 1955, would be followed, in the 1960s, by film and video footage of young Black protesters hosed by water cannons. The whole world watched as this revolution was born. This younger generation of Black individuals was willing to push back against the oppressive system, unlike the generation before them, because they saw no other way. Years of images of Black people had not changed. They were aware that their own image was beautiful, much as Douglass had hoped, but this was the time to shift how they were viewed in the nation. And it was going to take putting their Black skin in front of harm—and the camera—to do so.

Today pictures from our digital cameras pervade our social media feeds—and our attention. The cameras embedded in our handy cell phones have made it possible for every occasion and amusement to be captured. Yet it was also this technology that helped to spark a racial justice movement. An array of NASA-designed photodetectors, smaller than a thumbnail, sat ready to dispatch an image across the Internet, making it possible for any event to be seen across the globe in real time. It was with a cell phone camera that the video footage of the killing of George Floyd, like a modern-day lynching, became a flash point, much like that of Till a few decades earlier. This time was different, however, because the whole world witnessed it. This time the whole world reacted. This time marchers, both Black and white, cried out that Black Lives Matter. The cell phone camera recorded the misuse of power but also displayed to the protestors that they have their own.

For generations, Black Americans have raised their voices about the atrocities against them, using the technology of the time. And one of the ways they displayed racism was by using their Black figure in front of cameras to bring it into better relief. Many allies today have said they were not aware of their privilege or their racism, likening both of them to water for fish. The detection is no longer a mystery, however. Pictures have long provided proof of anti-Black racism, first starting as occasional disturbances in the water in the days of Douglass to the torrent of them flooding our cell phones today. But cameras and their photodetectors can only do so much. They can only bear witness. Once something is seen, the next step is not just to say something but to strategize, to reimagine the future and, most importantly, to act.

About the Author

Ainissa Ramirez, Ph.D., is a scientist and science communicator. A Brown and Stanford graduate, she has worked as a research scientist at Bell Labs and held academic positions at Yale University and MIT. She is the author of The Alchemy of Us *(The MIT Press, 2020).*

The Racist Legacy of Computer-Generated Humans

By Theodore Kim

Computer-generated imagery is supposed to be one of the success stories of computer science. Starting in the 1970s, the algorithms for realistically depicting digital worlds were developed in a monumental joint effort between academic, commercial and federal research labs. Today, we stream the results onto the screens in our homes. Escaping into worlds where computer-generated superheroes right all wrongs, or toys come to life to comfort us, are welcome respites from stories of real-life systemic racism, the ubiquitous dimensions of which are becoming clearer every day.

Alas, this technology has an insidious, racist legacy all its own.

For almost two decades, I have worked on the science and technology behind movies. I was formerly a senior research scientist at Pixar and am currently a professor at Yale. If you have seen a blockbuster movie in the last decade, you have seen my work. I got my start at Rhythm and Hues Studios in 2001, when the first credible computer-generated humans began appearing in film. The real breakthrough was the character of Gollum in *The Lord of the Rings: The Two Towers* (2002), when Weta Digital applied a technique from Stanford called "dipole approximation" that convincingly captured the translucency of his skin. For the scientists developing these technologies, the term "skin" has become synonymous with "translucency." Decades of effort has been poured into faithfully capturing this phenomenon.

However, translucency is only the dominating visual feature in *young, white* skin. Entwining the two phenomena is akin to calling pink Band-Aids "flesh-colored." Surveying the technical literature on digital humans is a stomach-churning tour of whiteness. Journal articles on "skin rendering" often feature a single image

Section 5: Racism in Science and Technology

of a computer-generated white person as empirical proof that the algorithm can depict "humans."

This technical obsession with youthful whiteness is a direct reflection of Hollywood appetites. As in real life, the roles for computer-generated humans all go to young, white thespians. Consider: a youthful Arnold Schwarzenegger in *Terminator Salvation* (2009), a young Jeff Bridges in *Tron: Legacy* (2010), a de-aged Orlando Bloom in *The Hobbit: The Desolation of Smaug* (2013), Arnold again in *Terminator Genisys* (2015), a youthful Sean Young in *Blade Runner: 2049* (2017), and a 1980s-era Carrie Fisher in both *Rogue One: A Star Wars Story* (2017) and *Star Wars: The Rise of Skywalker* (2019).

The technological white supremacy extends to human hair, where the term "hair" has become shorthand for the visual features that dominate white people's hair. The standard model for rendering hair, the "Marschner" model, was custom-designed to capture the subtle glints that appear when light interacts with the micro-structures in flat, straight hair. No equivalent micro-structural model has ever been developed for kinky, Afro-textured hair. In practice, the straight-hair model just gets applied as a good-enough hand-me-down.

Similarly, algorithms for simulating the *motion* of hair assume that it is composed of straight or wavy fibers locally sliding over each other. This assumption does not hold for kinky hair, where each follicle is in persistent collision with a global range of follicles all over the scalp. Over the last two decades, I have never seen an algorithm developed to handle this case.

This racist state of technology was not inevitable. The 2001 space-opera flop *Final Fantasy: The Spirits Within* was released before the dipole approximation was available. The main character, Dr. Aki Ross, is a young, fair-skinned scientist of ambiguous ethnicity, and much of the movie's failure was placed on her distressingly hard and plasticine-looking skin. Less often mentioned was the fact that two other characters in the movie, the Black space marine Ryan Whittaker and the elderly Dr. Sid, looked much more realistic than Aki Ross. Blacker and older skin does not require as much translucency to appear lifelike. If the filmmakers had aligned their art with the limitations of the technology, Aki Ross should have been modeled after a latter-day Eartha Kitt.

For a brief moment in the 2000s, the shortest scientific path to achieving realistic digital humans was to refine the depiction of computer-generated Blackness in film, not to double down on algorithmic whiteness. Imagine the timeline that could have been. Instead of two more decades of computer-animated whiteness, a generation of moviegoers could have seen their own humanity radiating from Black heroes. That alternate timeline is gone; we live in this one instead.

Today's moviemaking technology has been built to tell white stories, because researchers working at the intersection of art and science have allowed white flesh and hair to insidiously become the only form of humanity considered worthy of in-depth scientific inquiry. Going forward, we need to ask whose stories this technology is furthering. What cases have been treated as "normal," and which are "special"? How many humans reside in those cases, and why?

The racist legacy of computer-generated imagery does not cost people their lives, but it determines whose stories can be told. And if Black Lives Matter, then the stories of their lives must matter too.

About the Author

Theodore Kim is an associate professor in the Department of Computer Science at Yale University and the recipient of a Scientific and Technical Academy Award.

Section 6: Overcoming Racism

6.1 How to Unlearn Racism
 By Abigail Libers

6.2 Charles Blow Tells You How to Actually Fight Racism
 By Bernadette Bynoe

6.3 To Fight Bias, Consider Highlighting Your Race or Gender
 By Erika Kirgios, Aneesh Rai, Edward Chang and Katy Milkman

6.4 We'll Never Fix Systemic Racism by Being Polite
 By Aldon Morris

How to Unlearn Racism

By Abigail Libers

In February 2016 I sat in a conference room on the Upper East Side of Manhattan with about 35 other people attempting to answer what seemed like a straightforward question: *What is racism?*

I—a white, able-bodied, cis-gendered woman in my 30s—thought that racism was prejudice against an individual because of race or ethnicity. That's why I had signed up for the Undoing Racism Workshop, a two-and-a-half-day antiracist training that analyzes race and power structures in the U.S.: I wanted to gain a better understanding of why some people have so much contempt toward those who are different from them. My yearning for answers came from personal experience with discrimination as a Jewish woman and the daughter of immigrants; my parents fled to the U.S. from the former Soviet Union in 1979. Growing up in a small town in upstate New York followed by an even smaller, more rural town in Georgia, I was picked on and often felt "othered."

The workshop was hosted by the People's Institute for Survival and Beyond (PISAB), an organization that was founded 40 years ago by community organizers who wanted to create a more equitable society by addressing the root causes of racism. Our leaders—a Black man, a white woman and a Latina woman—called on each of us to share our definitions of racism. People's responses were all over the map, from "a mean-spirited, close-minded way of thinking" to "discrimination based on someone's skin color or ethnic background." The trainers validated each of our responses before pointing out how varied they were and explaining that few of us had identified racism as a web of institutional power and oppression based on skin color. Not having a simple or agreed-on definition of racism makes it easier to keep racism in place. To undo racism, they said, we need a common language that ties together individual and systemic factors. Hearing racism described as a power hierarchy was eye-opening for me. Having been marginalized myself, I thought

Section 6: Overcoming Racism

I was sensitive toward other groups who faced discrimination. I thought I got it.

Over the past year, America has been reckoning with racism on a scale that has not been seen since the civil rights movement. The killings of George Floyd, Ahmaud Arbery, Breonna Taylor and others sparked protests against systemic racism and police violence that have drawn multiracial participation. Some white Americans attended Black Lives Matter protests for the first time—the movement has been active since 2013—and saw up close the police brutality they previously only read about or witnessed through short video clips on phone screens. These experiences were a tiny window into the reality of violence and oppression that Black people endure. The pandemic further emphasizes the racial disparities that people are protesting, with Black, Latinx and Indigenous communities disproportionately affected by COVID-19. It has become widely discussed that police violence and virus deaths are not disparate issues—they are both embedded in a pervasive system of racism.

PISAB's definition of racism (which is similar to that of other antiracism organizations such as the Racial Equity Institute) is race prejudice plus power. It describes how individual and systemic racism are tied together. All of us have individual race prejudice: anyone can prejudge a person based on race alone. But what makes racism different from individual prejudice is who has institutional power. White people control our government systems and institutions in every sector, from law enforcement and education to health care and the media, leading to laws and policies that can advantage white people while disadvantaging everyone else.

White people's dominance in our systems is why you may have heard people refer to the U.S. as a white supremacist society. In this context, white supremacy does not refer to hate groups such as neo-Nazis and the Ku Klux Klan but rather an entire system where one group has all the advantages. "Racism is white supremacy," says Joseph Barndt, an organizer and core trainer with PISAB and author of *Understanding and Dismantling Racism: The Twenty-First*

Century Challenge to White America. "It's empowering one alleged racial group over another and creating systems to reinforce that."

As more white people seek to confront and undo racism in their own lives, they are figuring out how to "do the work." In recent years implicit bias trainings, which aim to expose people to the negative associations and stereotypes they hold and express unconsciously, have been widely used to raise people's awareness of racism in workplaces. But addressing bias is not sufficient for confronting the racist systems, ideas and legacies that are present in our day-to-day lives. There is no one-size-fits-all solution, but research shows that undoing racism often starts with understanding what race and racism actually are. It is also crucial to develop a positive racial identity; to feel—not just intellectualize—how racism harms all of us and, finally, to learn how to break prejudice habits and become an active antiracist. Doing so, however, is not accomplished in a weekend. For me, one of the first steps was unlearning false ideas about the basis of racial categories.

Seeing Whiteness in the Origins of Race

Race is deeply embedded in our society, yet it is persistently misunderstood to be a biological construct rather than a cultural one. The concept of racial categories is actually quite modern, explains Crystal Fleming, a professor of sociology at Stony Brook University and author of *How to Be Less Stupid about Race*:"If we think about our species existing for at least a few hundred thousand years, it's only in the last several centuries that we see the historical emergence of the idea of race." This is a history that most Americans are not taught in school.

False classifications of humans that would later be called "races" began in the 16th and 17th centuries with Christian clergy questioning whether "Blacks" and "Indians" were human. As colonial expansion and slavery increased, religion was used to justify classifying Black people and other people of color as "pagan and soulless." But as many of them were converted to Christianity

Section 6: Overcoming Racism

and the Age of Enlightenment took off in the 1700s, religion lost its legitimizing power.

Instead "science" was used to justify the enslavement of Africans and the genocide of Indigenous peoples, which had already been occurring in British colonies for more than a century. Johann Friedrich Blumenbach, a German anthropologist and comparative anatomist, is known for proposing one of the earliest classifications of the human race, which he wrote about in the late 1700s.

His measurement of skulls from around the world led him to divide humans into five groups, which were later simplified by anthropologists into three categories: Caucasoids, Mongoloids and Negroids. It did not seem to matter that some prominent scientists, including Charles Darwin, dismissed a biological basis for race over the next century. Many scientists dedicated themselves to proving a false racial hierarchy in which "Caucasians" were superior to other races.

In the U.S., political and intellectual leaders reinforced the false ideology that Africans were biologically inferior to other races and therefore best suited for slavery. After Bacon's Rebellion in 1676, which had united white and Black indentured servants, Virginia lawmakers began to make legal distinctions between "white" and "Black" people. Poor white indentured servants who served their term could go free and own land; Black servants were committed to lifelong servitude. With the Naturalization Act of 1790, Congress codified white racial advantage into law by limiting citizenship by naturalization to "free white persons," namely white men. Women, people of color and indentured servants were excluded.

With white superiority cemented firmly into law, the social and political power of *whiteness* was born. As a category, it was increasingly associated with resources and power: explicit laws and practices that created whiteness as a requirement for being able to live in certain neighborhoods, to be able to vote, to own land, to testify in court before a jury. The legacy of "scientific" racism persists to this day.

Although biology has shown that there are no genetically distinct races, racial *identity*—how you and others perceive your race—is very real, as are its ramifications. In a white-dominant society like America, white people tend to be unaware of their identity and may think of themselves as neutral, as nonracial. According to the work of psychologist Janet Helms, who published six stages of white racial identity development in 1999, the first stage is defined by a lack of awareness of cultural and institutional racism. This stage is also characterized by being "color-blind"—imagining one does not see people's differences and viewing that as a positive trait others should aspire to.

As scholar and activist Peggy McIntosh notes in a 1989 article, this lack of awareness is common. She describes white privilege as an "invisible package of unearned assets that I can count on cashing in each day, but about which I was 'meant' to remain oblivious. White privilege is like an invisible weightless knapsack of special provisions, maps, passports, codebooks, visas, clothes, tools, and blank checks."

To unlearn racism then, white people must first examine their racial identity. Black scholars and writers of color have known this for more than a century; their survival depended on it. Frederick Douglass, W.E.B. Du Bois, James Baldwin, Audre Lorde, Angela Davis, Ta-Nehisi Coates and many others have observed, analyzed and written about whiteness for generations. Du Bois made observations about whiteness in 1899 with his sociological study *The Philadelphia Negro* and in 1935 with his book, *Black Reconstruction in America*. Recently Ijeoma Oluo, author of *So You Want to Talk about Race*, wrote in a popular Medium article: "I know white culture better than most white people know white culture."

It has only been in the past few decades that white scholars have turned the lens on themselves with the emergence of Critical Whiteness Studies (CWS), a growing academic field that aims to examine the structures of white supremacy and privilege and to investigate the meaning of white privilege and how it is connected to complicity in racism. According to Barbara Applebaum, a professor of philosophy and education at Syracuse University, CWS shifts the focus, and thus the blame, from the victims of racism to the perpetrators. As she explains, "it names the elephant in the room—the construction and maintenance of whiteness."

Workshops Aren't Enough

Over the past 20 years or so initiatives to address racism have focused heavily on implicit bias trainings. A growing body of cognitive research demonstrates how these hidden biases impact our attitudes and actions, which result in real-world consequences such as racial profiling.

The trainings, which are often sponsored by human resources departments but delivered to employees by outside consulting firms, may consist of modules that walk people through what implicit bias is and where it comes from, how it shows up in the workplace, how it is measured (typically through the Implicit Association Test) and how to reduce it. Over the past decade these trainings have been widely used in the law-enforcement industry as well as in the tech industry, with companies such as Facebook and Google putting thousands of employees through trainings. More recently, antibias trainings have been implemented in schools for teachers.

While these sessions may be useful in exposing people's hidden biases, those revelations have not been shown to result in long-term behavioral change on an individual or systemic level. In a 2018 paper published in *Anthropology Now*, Harvard University sociologist Frank Dobbin writes: "Hundreds of studies dating back to the 1930s suggest that antibias training does not reduce bias, alter behavior or change the workplace."

A recent meta-analysis of 492 studies (with a total of 87,418 participants) on the effectiveness of implicit bias training found weak effects on unconscious bias. The authors note that "most studies focused on producing short-term changes with brief, single-session manipulations" and that most trainings "produced trivial changes in behavior." The authors conclude that changes in implicit bias are possible, but they do not necessarily translate into changes in explicit bias or behavior, and there is a significant lack of research on the long-term effects.

"Implicit bias trainings raise awareness, but they also tell people, 'This is just how the brain works,'" says Rachel Godsil, co-founder and co-director of the Perception Institute, an organization that works with social scientists to identify the efficacy of interventions to address implicit bias, racial anxiety and the effects of stereotypes. "It kind of leaves people feeling like they are let off the hook." It's not that your brain is hard-wired to be racist, but it *is* programmed to put people into categories. And the categories that have been constructed in the U.S., Godsil explains, have meanings that tend to be negative for people from marginalized groups. She emphasizes that part of what it means to unlearn racism is to delink stereotypes from identities and absolute truths: "You're not trying to be color-blind or pretend that these categories don't exist, but you don't presume you know anything about a person based on their identity."

Antiracism trainings, such as the Undoing Racism Workshop, differ significantly from implicit bias trainings in that they are more intense on both an intellectual and emotional level. Because they are not done in a corporate setting, the discussions tend to be more honest and raw. In the PISAB training I attended, we took a hard look at white supremacy and our role in upholding it. After reviewing a history of racism in the U.S., the trainers discussed individual and institutional racial attitudes, oppression and privilege, and how institutions implicitly or explicitly perpetuate racism. We were empowered to be "gatekeepers"—leaders who can affect change in our workplaces and communities.

PISAB's methodology is rooted in community organizing principles that the group's founders honed for decades. Their approach is based on philosopher Paulo Freire's pedagogy, which focuses on linking knowledge to action so people can make real change in their communities. Other antiracist trainings, such as the one offered by Crossroads Antiracism Organizing & Training, provide a similar approach. In contrast, Robin DiAngelo, author of *White Fragility: Why It's So Hard for White People to Talk about Racism*,

Section 6: Overcoming Racism

who has received much attention in recent months, gives "keynote presentations" that are more focused on individual prejudice and white privilege.

Whereas these trainings can be powerful in many ways, it is unclear to what degree they are effective—and if they are, how and why they work. A 2015 study published in *Race and Social Problems* aimed to measure the impact of PISAB's training and found that approximately 60 percent of participants engaged in racial equity work after completing the Undoing Racism Workshop. "These trainings are well intentioned, but we don't know if they work, because there aren't randomized controlled experiments to prove that they do," says Patricia Devine, a professor of psychology who studies prejudice at the University of Wisconsin–Madison.

Trainings on implicit bias, diversity and antiracism may be limited in their efficacy in part because they tend to be brief one-off events. Promising research by Devine in 2013 showed that prejudices and biases can be more successfully unlearned through longer-term intervention. The 12-week longitudinal study was based on the premise that implicit bias is like a habit that can be broken through the following steps: becoming aware of implicit bias, developing concern about the effects of that bias and using strategies to reduce bias—specifically, ones that replace biased reactions with responses that reflect one's nonprejudiced goals.

The researchers argue that the motivation to "break the prejudice habit" comes from two sources: First, you have to be aware of your biases, and second, you have to be *concerned* about the consequences of your biases to be motivated to make the effort needed to eliminate them. Recent research has shown that interacting with a wide variety of racial groups can help people care more about racial justice. For instance, a 2018 review suggested that increased contact among racial groups deepens psychological investment in equality by making people more empathetic.

For Fleming, who has educated thousands of university students, teaching implicit bias within the context of a comprehensive, three-month course "is far more effective than being dragged into a diversity training for an afternoon," she says. "People have to feel inspired. They have to feel a desire to critically reflect on not just their biases but on their socialization and conditioning and to be part of a positive social transformation. You can't force that on anyone."

Feeling the Harms of Racism

The inspiration that Fleming speaks to is what motivates me to unlearn racism, to reeducate myself on swaths of American history, and to open my eyes to whiteness and white supremacy. But the process of unlearning is only the first step, and it needs to translate into a commitment to practices such as breaking white silence and bringing an antiracist lens to my work. That is only possible, and sustainable, by building empathy and *feeling* the ways in which racism is not just harmful for people of color—it hurts white people, too.

This realization didn't hit me until I took PISAB's workshop for a second time in 2019. I had signed up at the urging of Stoop Nilsson, a social worker and racial reeducation coach who shows white people how to become antiracist leaders in their communities. During the workshop, Barndt, one of the trainers, pointed out how easy it can be for white people to think racism does not harm them. But "the truth is, with racism we lose, too," he said. "All of humanity loses. With the end of racism, we get our lives back."

H. Shellae Versey, a critical health researcher and professor of psychology at Fordham University, studies how white supremacy culture impacts the mental health of both white and nonwhite populations. In a 2019 paper, she and her co-authors explain how white people are harmed by the myth of meritocracy—the idea that working hard and pulling yourself up by your bootstraps leads to success. When this does not happen (for example, if you do not land a promotion you worked hard for), it threatens your worldview and leads to significant stress, research shows.

Versey notes that many white people oppose social health programs such as the Affordable Care Act that would actually benefit them, in part because they believe these programs are designed to benefit people of color. In his recent book *Dying of Whiteness*, physician Jonathan Metzl writes about how some white Americans support politicians who promote policies that increase their risk of sickness and death.

Another way we are all harmed on a day-to-day basis is through white supremacy culture. As Kenneth Jones and Tema Okun write in the book *Dismantling Racism: A Workbook for Social Change Groups*, the characteristics of white supremacy culture include perfectionism, a sense of urgency, defensiveness, quantity over quality, paternalism, either/or thinking, power hoarding, individualism, and more.

Understanding and *feeling* how racism hurts me—even though it is a mere fraction of the pain people of color experience—is part of what helps me internalize the motivation I need to consistently work to undo it. I wonder if white supremacy culture contributes to my elevated anxiety levels, which manifest as migraine headaches and torn-up cuticles. I am more clearly connecting white supremacy culture with climate change denial as well as the paternalism and overly rigid thinking I have experienced in various jobs.

Working with Nilsson is helping me create a positive racial identity of my own—as both a white person and a Russian Jew. Our country prides itself on being a melting pot, but much gets lost in the assimilation to whiteness and white supremacy culture. Markers of ethnic identity such as language, food, culture and music are discouraged; those from a non–Western European heritage are often vilified. In my family, my parents were so committed to learning English that they hardly ever spoke Russian around the house. I never learned it. It saddens me that I can't speak to my own parents in their native language and that I still know so little about our heritage. Recently my mom became frustrated trying to remember a word in English to describe how she was feeling; I worry that her last words will be in Russian, and I'll have no idea what they mean.

In the midst of COVID-19, a high-stakes election season and racial protest movements that illuminate issues affecting everyone, many Americans are reevaluating what matters most. White people may be waking up to areas of their lives that were previously inaccessible to them and to histories and literature and legacies that have long been excluded from school curriculums. This awakening may lead people to work on creating a positive racial identity away from white supremacism, one based on fully acknowledging the power of whiteness in our society and using that knowledge to pursue equality and justice for everyone. Skipping that step risks giving up or doing even more harm; shame and self-loathing are not effective motivators and can inhibit the strength and stamina needed to push for systemic change.

Having been in this process myself for several years, I am certain of only one thing: that antiracism is a lifelong practice. In her book *Why Are All the Black Kids Sitting Together in the Cafeteria?*, psychologist Beverly Daniel Tatum compares racism to smog, writing that it is something we all breathe in; no one is immune to it. Attempting to unlearn racism has meant becoming aware of each inhalation—and doing my best to exhale less of it.

About the Author

Abigail Libers is a freelance journalist and editor based in New York.

Charles Blow Tells You How to Actually Fight Racism

By Bernadette Bynoe

How do we make real progress on racism? What does it take to face our own biases? How might we actually understand the perspectives and experiences of people whose sex, gender or ethnicity is different from our own?

"We need to see people other than ourselves in order to empathize. If we don't live around others, we do ourselves and our society damage—because our ability to relate becomes impaired," says Charles Blow, a *New York Times* columnist and author. "It's easy to demonize or simply dismiss people you don't know or see.... It's nearly impossible to commiserate with the unseen and unknown."

Similar thoughts have been running through the minds of many since the height of the Black Lives Matter (BLM) movement amid the backdrop of the global COVID pandemic. The Black Employee Network formed in 2020 at Springer Nature (*Scientific American*'s parent company) in answer to colleagues' calls for a forum for such discussions. With a global committee of seven, the network has begun addressing some of the thoughts and feelings of Black employees and allies. And it has started a conversation on diversity, equity and inclusion within scientific publishing and beyond.

In December 2020 the Springer Nature Black Employee Network and *Scientific American* kicked off this conversation with Blow as guest speaker. He talked about crucial issues, including police brutality during the ongoing COVID-19 pandemic, dealing with microaggressions, or subtly and often unconsciously prejudiced speech and behavior, and diversifying workplaces.

An edited transcript of the interview follows.

COVID-19 is disproportionately affecting Black, Hispanic and Indigenous communities. But members of minority groups

might mistrust vaccinations because of historical racism in health care. What are your thoughts on how these feelings will impact marginalized people in terms of eradicating the novel coronavirus?

There needs to be a well-funded, concerted campaign that's going to have to build trust within the Black community about COVID vaccines. For centuries, there are many examples in every generation about something catastrophic that happened to Black people that was facilitated by the government and instituted by the health care system. Some people look at that and think, "I don't trust any of it." And it prevents them from going to the hospital.

There is a disproportionate number of Black women who die in childbirth when they shouldn't be dying. Why? The doctors don't believe you when you tell them there is a problem. We need a campaign around the vaccine. But thinking more broadly, we have to deal with some of these structures. People are not making it up when they say they don't trust this system and they don't trust their doctors. If their doctor, like some studies show, refuses to prescribe pain medication to the same degree—because they don't believe that Black people feel pain in the same way—that's part of the issue. Pediatricians don't prescribe Black children the same level of pain medication as they do white kids because, subconsciously, they are not registering their pain in the same way.

Now, ironically, this is why white people disproportionately have the opioid problem. Distrust is not fabricated; it is based on horrible experiences that Black people had, and continue to have, in the medical field.

Regarding the police killings of George Floyd and Breonna Taylor: Do you think the pandemic has been a catalyst for added attention and calls for action despite such situations happening before?

The pivotal word in your question is "catalyst." Was it a catalyst or was it an excuse? Was the killing of George Floyd, and the protests that erupted after, a hall pass? People have been cooped up because

Section 6: Overcoming Racism

of the pandemic, and suddenly they could congregate and be with other human beings. As soon as things started to reopen in the fall, public support of Black Lives Matter began to go back down among white people in particular. Maybe once enough time has passed, we will understand what happened this summer. But the question remains: How real was it?

Pew [Research Center] did its polling of the people participating in the protests, and the vast majority of them were white. Where were they when other people were being killed? It's not just about learning some new things. In order to change the system of oppression, you're going to have to get uncomfortable. If the presence of Black culture and Hispanic culture makes you uncomfortable, that's what you need to feel because until you are willing to live your life in a space, in a community, in an environment that embraces every culture equally, you still have the problem. There's no set of books you're going to be able to read to undo that if you still want to live in a majority white neighborhood, so you can keep the majority white school. There's no amount of putting Black Lives Matter placards in your neighborhood if you have more BLM signs than you have Black people. That's not going to make it right.

In a segment on the CBS News program *Sunday Morning***, you said that you were 18 years old when a cop first pulled a gun on you. How do you think that kind of experience affects young men and women and their interactions with the police as they grow into older adults? How has it affected you?**

It's incredibly traumatic. The people who are supposed to protect you are the ones who are threatening your life. It really undermines your ability to have faith in the system. Who do Black people call [when they] have been the victim of this? When there's a problem, you are hesitant to call the police. I'm hesitant. We've seen people get killed because somebody calls the police to do a welfare check on someone who has a mental illness. Then the person ends up dead. So now that makes me far less likely to call the police to do a welfare check on somebody.

My brother recently passed away from an illness in his organs, but it was also affecting him mentally. And he was in his home, and my mother called the police, and I freaked out. All I can think is, "He's not going to be rational. And it's so easy to kill him, because he's suffering a medical illness that is leading to a mental problem." [This issue] undermines our ability to trust the system. It also, on a more practical level, inhibits a lot of Black people from joining the police force. It's hard to recruit me if you've been locking [me up], if you've been throwing me down and frisking me. It's hard to recruit me if you pull guns on me. If I consider you the gang, it's going to be hard for you to recruit me.

What are your thoughts on Black men and women who enter the police force to make a difference and change its impression on Black children?

First, I hope that's not why they have to do it. I'm from the South, and I grew up in a small, majority-Black town. We had one police officer; he was Black. Then he was replaced with a guy who was my cousin by marriage; he was Black. So I just never grew up with fear of police officers. I grew up thinking he had a great job, and he was protecting us—and that's how people should feel. I assume that's how white people feel about the police because I never felt like I was in danger. I never felt like they were going out of their way to pick on me. This was your neighbor. They weren't trying to bother you. They weren't trying to make money for the city by giving you a fine.

I appreciate law enforcement done right—which is that it's empathetic, that it is character-driven. It is moral. It is not a profit-making entity. It is not brutal without repercussion. It is not racially skewed in its targeting. And that can exist. But in big cities, [law enforcement has] become an entity unto itself. Even when a city's police force is more diverse or even majority-Black, often the union is white. The power structure is white. There is corruption in that system. So that doesn't mean that you don't need structures that make sure the laws get obeyed, because we all need a civil society.

Section 6: Overcoming Racism

But what we have created is a law-enforcement structure that is itself uncivil.

What role does the media play in the perception of Black people?

In general, research shows that we are more likely to be portrayed in the media in the criminal sense. We're less likely to have redemptive narratives. For example, when you're a victim of something, and the media says, "He was a choirboy" or "He was a valedictorian" or "He was captain of the football team"—those redemptive, humanizing qualities are less likely to be ascribed to Black people when either they are the victim or the perpetrator in a news story.

Victimization is generally reserved for white people, particularly white women. There was a phenomenon we in the news business used to talk about: missing white woman syndrome. The prettier the person was—in white people's definition of beauty—and the younger they were, the bigger the story was. A missing white woman is a huge story.

Black women also go missing every day. Black children go missing every day. When's the last time you heard a story, on the level of JonBenet Ramsey, of a Black girl missing? That is probably a holdover from the beginning of the country. White femininity has always been used as an activator of white power structures. It was used to lynch. It was used to burn down whole communities. Some people don't realize that the Tulsa massacre, which they called race riots, happened because a white woman said that a young Black man in the elevator had done something to her. So the media plays a huge role in this kind of idolizing of white victimhood and brandishing of Black criminality.

How do you think the protests have affected the workplace in terms of interactions among Black colleagues, other people of color and white colleagues?

It's hard to really gauge that because we have all been working from home for months. I do believe that there were a lot of conversations had. But if you look across the spectrum, there was a knee-jerk reaction. All of a sudden, everybody has the diversity initiative. All of a sudden, everybody's assigning books to read. Black people get shows; books race up the best-seller list. People who do talks like this, like me, get a zillion requests, all of that activity. But having lived in this Black body for 50 years, I've seen these knee-jerk reactions before. And I know that the knee eventually falls back into place. So I'm always looking to figure out how much of this is a true commitment to diversity and a sustained sense of equality and how much of it is to ward off the possibility of disruption.

Sometimes what people describe as a period of unity is actually a period of silence. When people are quiet about their discomfort and their oppression and their pain, people call that racial ease, racial unity. But as soon as you start to vocalize that you are not happy with your oppression, they call that racial unrest. They call that racial issues, racial friction. And what they're really trying to address is your objection, not the system that is making you object.

Always remember that racism is not really about attitudes, although attitude is a part of racism. The primary instrument of racism is power. It is the power to have advantages over you in workplaces, in social environments and every other place. It is the power to have an economic advantage over you. When you see people trying to disenfranchise voters, that's all about power. When you see people locking up certain citizens, that's about the power to not have you in their space.

In "Constructing a Conversation on Race," published in the *New York Times* in 2014, you wrote, "A true racial dialogue is not intra-racial but interracial.... Data must be presented. Experiences must be explored. Histories and systems must be laid bare. Biases, fears, stereotype and mistrust must be examined." What important steps should companies take to ensure the conversation continues and effectively allows voices to be heard?

The conversation is about white supremacy and how it has always operated in America—and how it operates in corporate America, how it operates in medical fields, how it operates in the criminal justice system, how it operates in education. I am not on equal footing; my ancestor was not on equal footing. We came to this conversation from different perspectives.

I am always struck by how, whenever I'm having a discussion or giving a speech about racism and inequality and white supremacy, the majority of the people that I'm speaking to are Black. I'm speaking to the wrong crowd. Why is this room not filled with white people? Because, in general, it is considered to be our problem. What kind of sense does that make? We need to sit around and talk about our oppression? No, the people with the power need to be sitting around talking about it. What are you going to do?

And people act like Black people have some kind of magical insight into this. No, we don't. There's no racial information on our birth certificate that tells us how to navigate racism in America. We don't get an extra set of school books in school that teach us how to learn history about racism and how to deal with it. We have to learn it on our own over a whole lifetime. You need to do the same thing! If you're not putting in the work and trying to figure out how to deal with this and how to get rid of it, you're not serious. I've done the work my whole life trying to figure out well, you expect me to give you five bullet points to change the world? It doesn't work that way.

To Fight Bias, Consider Highlighting Your Race or Gender

By Erika Kirgios, Aneesh Rai, Edward Chang and Katy Milkman

A friend (let's call her Rosa) recently spent several weeks cold-e-mailing business school alumni who had built successful ventures. Rosa is a woman of color and an aspiring entrepreneur, and she planned to apply to business school herself. She hoped to build her network or at least get some useful advice. But she faced a dilemma: In her messages, should she highlight that she's a woman and a member of a racial minority group in entrepreneurship—or let her identity fade into the background?

We were also curious. After all, Rosa's identity might help her stand out in a positive way, or it could trigger a prejudiced response. So we decided to do some research. We surveyed 200 people who identified as women or members of racial or ethnic minority groups to ask what they would do in Rosa's shoes. Only 35 percent told us they would highlight their identity in requests for career support. Rosa herself, who ultimately decided not to mention her identity, articulated a concern that many of our respondents shared: "I'm worried I'll come off as needy or seeking attention or like I'm playing this 'race' or 'female' card if I mention my identity explicitly."

These fears are reasonable. Several decades of experiments have shown that women and members of racial minority groups whose name signals their identity typically receive fewer responses than white men to otherwise identical e-mails or job applications. Just signing an e-mail as "Amanda Cabot," "Alma Hernandez" or "Deshawn Washington" leads people to assume that they know your race, ethnicity or gender. If the signature alone makes someone less likely to respond to a message, it's sensible to worry that drawing extra attention to your marginalized identity can only make things worse.

Section 6: Overcoming Racism

But our recent research suggests the opposite is often true. We have found that explicitly mentioning your underrepresented identity when seeking career help can be beneficial.

We first tested this idea in a large experiment with local elected offcials. We sent networking e-mails to 2,476 white, male city councilmen from 701 U.S. cities, including giant ones such as New York City and smaller ones such as Bentonville, Ark. Our e-mails appeared to come from students who said they wanted advice about going into politics. (In reality, these students were fictitious.) We varied the senders, using names that suggested they were white men (e.g., "Hunter Anderson"), white women (e.g., "Abigail Miller"), Black men (e.g., "Tyrone Robinson"), Black women (e.g., "Aliyah Harris"), Latinos (e.g., "Alejandro Gutierrez") or Latinas (e.g., "Camila Rodriguez"). All the e-mails were identical except that some messages explicitly mentioned the fictional sender's identity and others did not.

We sent our e-mails on a Tuesday morning. Within one week, about a third of the contacted politicians had replied. Response rates to e-mails from names perceived as belonging to white men were similar, whether they referred to themselves as a "young person" or referenced their gender by describing themselves as a "young man." (We did not use e-mails that directly referred to white senders' racial identity because preliminary tests suggested that recipients would associate such messages with white nationalism.)

Things got more interesting when we analyzed responses to messages from women and racial or ethnic minority group members. When female or minority senders explicitly mentioned their identities, they were just more than 24 percent more likely to receive a response, compared with e-mails that had the same signature but did not mention identities. E-mails that mentioned identities received higher-quality replies, too: politicians wrote responses that were about 32 percent longer and about 39 percent more likely to offer to set up a phone call or meeting.

Strikingly, mentioning identity had the biggest benefit for Black men. Politicians were about 60 percent more likely to respond to messages from Black men when they asked councilmen to write back with "a few words of wisdom for a young Black man hoping to one day become a city councilor, like you." This effect held regardless of the politicians' ideological leaning or proximity to reelection. Moreover mentioning identity was just as likely to benefit women and members of racial or ethnic minority groups in cities that voted for Donald Trump in 2016 as in cities that voted for Hillary Clinton. And the effect persisted regardless of the city's size, demographic diversity or wealth.

These effects extend beyond politicians. In another experiment, we sent 1,169 undergraduates at an Ivy League university an e-mail from a (fictitious) Black, male graduate student named Demarcus Rivers, who asked for help with his dissertation research. Regardless of the recipients' gender, race or political leaning, when Demarcus described himself as "a Black man working towards a Ph.D.," students were almost twice as likely to volunteer to help him.

Why is it so important to mention that you're "a woman in STEM" or "a Black man pursuing a law degree"? Our research suggests that drawing attention to your marginalized identity or minority status reminds people on the receiving end of your message that bias could influence their decision-making. That reminder, in turn, may motivate them to monitor their own reaction more closely and behave more helpfully. Most Americans want to avoid appearing or feeling prejudiced, whether that avoidance is to uphold their values or reputation. Helping someone who explicitly identifies as part of an underrepresented or disadvantaged community feels like an opportunity to prove to yourself or others that you support women and racial and ethnic minority groups and are therefore not prejudiced. A rosy read of our results would be that people just need a little nudge to behave in line with their values.

But prejudice exists, and it does have negative effects on people's professional lives. Work by other researchers suggests that women and members of racial minority groups whose name or curriculum vitae gives away their identity can benefit from hiding their gender or race when they are evaluated for a job. For example, one study found that Asian applicants fared better in U.S. job searches when they "Americanized" their name and interests, changing their name from "Lei" to "Luke," for example, or citing popular Western hobbies such as snowboarding.

This finding might seem to contradict our research. But a more accurate interpretation is that these studies all point to the dangers of allowing one's name alone to convey identity. Because sexism, racism and other forms of bias are all too common in the workplace, a signature that leaks your identity can trigger stereotypes that lead to discriminatory behavior. Concealing your identity can block the stereotyping process before it begins. Our work, meanwhile, offers another strategy to address the same problem. By highlighting your identity, you can prompt people to actively identify and suppress their potentially prejudiced responses.

The onus of reducing discrimination should not be on women and people of color. But in a world where inequity and bias are commonplace, having a tool to blunt these barriers may come in handy.

About the Authors

Erika Kirgios is a doctoral candidate in the Operations, Information and Decisions Department at the Wharton School at the University of Pennsylvania. She studies the decision-making biases that underlie inequality and designs interventions to improve outcomes for women and members of racial and ethnic minority groups.

Aneesh Rai is a doctoral candidate in the Operations, Information and Decisions Department at the Wharton School at the University of Pennsylvania. He researches factors that contribute to a lack of diversity in organizations, as well as interventions to help organizations become more diverse.

Edward Chang is an assistant professor of negotiation, organizations and markets at Harvard Business School. He researches evidence-based solutions to increase diversity, equity and inclusion in organizations.

Katy Milkman is a behavioral scientist and the James G. Dinan Professor of Operations, Information and Decisions at the Wharton School at the University of Pennsylvania. She is also the author of the book How to Change: The Science of Getting from Where You Are to Where You Want to Be, *host of the podcast* Choiceology *and co-director of the Behavior Change for Good Initiative.*

We'll Never Fix Systemic Racism by Being Polite

By Aldon Morris

Polarized America agrees on one thing: that the current round of protests against racist police violence may indeed force real reform. Former president Donald Trump said that protesters want to "overthrow the American Revolution" and that the National Guard and regular military must act decisively to "dominate the streets." Black Lives Matter activists worry that these protests, like so many over the past few decades, will eventually subside, leaving temporary concessions, symbolic victories and an unaltered regime of systemic racism, along with unabated police violence.

History shows us that Trump and others like him have some reason for fear—not of an actual rebellion but of a revolution that could overturn the racism that still pervades American society. Starting in the 1950s and continuing until the 1970s, civil rights protests overthrew the century-long and deeply embedded Jim Crow system in the South. How they accomplished this can offer important lessons for those intent on making Trump's fears come true.

In his 1963 "Letter from Birmingham Jail," Martin Luther King, Jr., succinctly summarized what he hoped the Birmingham campaign needed to accomplish to force durable structural change: "The purpose of our direct action program is to create a situation so crisis packed that it will inevitably open the door to negotiation."

These words were written in the midst of a comprehensive and sustained struggle to create chronic disruption in the city of Birmingham. Large contingents of protesters marched into—and refused to leave—the major downtown department stores; conducted sit-ins in virtually every inch of public space; and clogged all the major thoroughfares in the city. No customers could enter stores, no goods could be delivered, and no business was being conducted. The effort by public safety commissioner Bull Connor to "dominate the streets" using barbaric police violence against the demonstrators failed; instead it provoked even more disruption and larger protests. And further arrests were impossible because every jail in the city was filled far beyond capacity.

As King had predicted while incarcerated for his participation in these protests, a crisis-packed situation was achieved. And as soon as the business leaders and political elite realized that the demonstrations were indeed chronic, they negotiated with movement leaders, agreeing to dismantle racial segregation in commerce and public services.

These crisis-packed protests led to the eradication of Jim Crow laws and "Whites Only" signs and ultimately gave way to a regime change across the South. The creation of crisis-packed situations across the South resulted in the enactment of the 1964 Civil Rights Act and the 1965 Voting Rights Act. As I write in my book *The Origins of the Civil Rights Movement*, contrary to the sanitized, rose-colored-glasses version of history, change was not generated through nondisruptive marches of people singing "We Shall Overcome." Whether the Black Lives Matter movement creates meaningful and lasting change depends on the degree to which it disrupts regimes of racial inequalities and can sustain that disruption until the captains of white supremacy are ready to negotiate.

The movement has made a good start toward creating and sustaining crisis-packed situations across the U.S. Triggered by the killing of George Floyd in Minnesota, mass demonstrations in every state and scores of other countries have been disrupting "business as usual" in virtually every realm of life. On the ground in countless cities, the movement has been replicating King's Birmingham strategy, filling streets and shopping areas with protests that prevent access to stores, interfere with deliveries and drive away customers, creating—in the midst of the massive disruption caused by the COVID-19 pandemic—a chronic crisis in business districts.

The protests are disrupting police routines—including their routine use of excessive violence against communities of color—and forcing them to restrain their wrongdoing in confronting legitimate protest. The confrontations between police and protesters have produced high-profile police misconduct that has led, as it did in Birmingham, to larger and more disruptive protests, promising to create the chronic crisis that King prescribed as the necessary prerequisite for meaningful negotiation.

The protests have dominated television, print and radio news cycles and have riveted attention on systemic racism. New voices and ideas are penetrating the media and disrupting the ingrained loyalty to many of the cultural practices and symbols endorsing and enforcing racism. Protesters have toppled and removed Confederate monuments from public places, gaining, for the first time in decades, the attention of major media and forcing government and private institutions to remove symbols of white supremacy from public display.

The protests have disrupted America's claim to moral leadership in global affairs, especially when Trump advocated and acted—as he did in Lafayette Park in Washington, D.C.—to "dominate the streets" with military attacks on those protesting violent police assaults. And like Connor's efforts in Alabama nearly 60 years ago, these attacks have failed, producing larger and more disruptive protests.

So far the disruptions have yielded symbolic changes, including changing flags, replacing monuments, renaming buildings and streets, amending music lyrics and altering our vocabulary of discourse. These changes are hard-won and important, but the eradication of these symbols of white supremacy does not ameliorate the material hardship of systemic racism. They are the first concessions granted because they are not expensive. The toppling of Confederate statues can produce hurt feelings, humiliation and even homicidal rage among those who cherish the symbols of white supremacy, but they do not cost billions of dollars.

The structural changes that can reduce or eradicate systemic racism are altogether different from cultural changes. They require the reallocation of basic resources to equalize income and wealth, employment and underemployment, educational opportunities, incarceration rates and access to quality health care.

Structural changes are very expensive to implement, and they involve a zero-sum logic that places powerful institutions on the wrong side of history. They involve transferring money currently earmarked for police weaponry to underfunded schools in Black communities; slashing the military budget to finance low-income housing; and taxing obscene levels of executive pay and bloated corporate profits to make the minimum wage a living wage. To achieve structural changes, widespread and sustained social disruptions must continue until the powerful people and institutions whose funds are needed for equalization are ready to negotiate.

This is a unique moment in American history. The crucial question is whether current or future white and Black leaders of these powerful institutions appreciate that chronic crisis can only be ended if they negotiate the changes needed to move the country toward the democratic ideals it put on paper centuries ago. There are glimmers of hope that the current protests have been sufficient to compel negotiations that have already led to some reforms (outlawing choke holds, for example) and put more on the table for the first time, such as defunding the police. If these initial signs do not mature into systemic reform, then national crisis-packed disruption will be needed to move the U.S. toward a more perfect union.

About the Author

Aldon Morris is the Leon Forrest Professor of Sociology and African American Studies at Northwestern University and a previous president of the American Sociological Association. His landmark books include The Origins of the Civil Rights Movement *(The Free Press, 1986) and* The Scholar Denied: W.E.B. Du Bois and the Birth of Modern Sociology *(University of California Press, 2015).*

GLOSSARY

agency In sociology, the ability of a person to exert power or to fulfill their potential.

algorithm A procedure or system of rules for solving a problem.

anathema Describes a person or thing that is intensely disliked.

antipathy A deep dislike or aversion to something or someone.

antiracism A position that is deliberately opposed to racism.

catalyze To cause something to happen; to inspire.

cisgender Describes a person whose gender identity corresponds to their birth sex.

cognitive Having to do with intellectual abilities such as thinking and remembering.

cortisol A hormone produced by humans that, among other things, helps to control stress.

cultural racism The belief that the cultures of particular ethnic or racial groups are superior or inferior to those of other racial or ethnic groups.

daguerreotype A photograph taken using an early photographic process.

de-escalation A response to a conflict that is meant to prevent the conflict from escalating (getting worse).

ethnicity Belonging to a group that shares a national or cultural background.

existential Having to do with existence: for example, an existential threat is a threat to the existence of a person.

genocide The systematic destruction of a particular ethnic, racial or political group.

Glossary

ideology A system of beliefs about the world that is typical of a particular individual or group.

implicit bias A bias one holds against a person or group that one holds without being aware of it.

institutional racism Racism that exists in the laws, policies or regulations of a society or institution.

linguistic Having to do with language.

pedagogy A method or practice of teaching.

socioeconomic Having to do with social and economic factors.

FURTHER INFORMATION

Blackstock, Uché. "What the COVID-19 Pandemic Means for Black Americans," *Scientific American*, April 7, 2020, https://blogs.scientificamerican.com/voices/what-the-covid-19-pandemic-means-for-black-americans/.

Iwai, Yoshiko. "Medical Schools Need to Get Better at Addressing Structural Racism," *Scientific American*, August 2, 2020, https://www.scientificamerican.com/article/medical-schools-need-to-get-better-at-addressing-structural-racism/.

Morris, Aldon. "From Civil Rights to Black Lives Matter," *Scientific American*, February 3, 2021, https://www.scientificamerican.com/article/from-civil-rights-to-black-lives-matter1/.

Ogbunu, C. Brandon. "For Scientific Institutions, Racial Reconciliation Requires Reparations," *Scientific American*, June 12, 2020, https://www.scientificamerican.com/article/for-scientific-institutions-racial-reconciliation-requires-reparations/.

Ranganathan, Meghana, Julia Wilcots, Rohini Shivamoggi and Diana Dumit. "America's Maps Are Full of Racial Slurs—and That Needs to Change," *Scientific American*, March 30, 2021, https://www.scientificamerican.com/article/americas-maps-are-full-of-racial-slurs-and-that-needs-to-change/.

Schwartz, Jen, and Dan Schlenoff. "Reckoning with Our Mistakes," *Scientific American*, September 1, 2020, https://www.scientificamerican.com/article/reckoning-with-our-mistakes/.

Strings, Sabrina, and Lindo Bacon. "The Racist Roots of Fighting Obesity," *Scientific American*, June 4, 2020, https://www.scientificamerican.com/article/the-racist-roots-of-fighting-obesity2/.

CITATIONS

1.1 The Concept of "Race" Is a Lie by Peter G. Prontzos (May 14, 2019); 1.2 Buried Prejudice: The Bigot in Your Brain by Siri Carpenter (April 1, 2008); 1.3 How to Think About Implicit Bias by Keith Payne, Laura Niemi and John M. Doris (March 27, 2018); 1.4 The Flexibility of Racial Bias by Mina Cikara and Jay Van Bavel (June 2, 2015); 1.5 Microaggressions: Death by a Thousand Cuts by Derald Wing Sue (March 30, 2021); 2.1 Inequality Before Birth Contributes to Health Inequality in Adults by Janet Currie (October 1, 2020); 2.2 How Doctors Can Confront Racial Bias in Medicine by Rachel Pearson (November 1, 2015); 2.3 To Achieve Mental Health Equity, Dismantle Social Injustice by Ruth S. Shim and Sarah Y. Vinson (March 29, 2021); 2.4 Why Racism, Not Race, Is a Risk Factor for Dying of COVID-19 by Claudia Wallis (June 12, 2020); 2.5 Teaching Antiracism to the Next Generation of Doctors by Rupinder Kaur Legha (October 21, 2020); 3.1 A Civil Rights Expert Explains the Social Science of Police Racism by Lydia Denworth and Alexis J. Hoag (June 4, 2020); 3.2 How to Reduce Police Violence by Dina Fine Maron (July 22, 2016); 3.3 Police Violence Calls for Measures Beyond De-Escalation Training by Stacey McKenna (June 17, 2020); 3.4 I Can't Breathe: Asthma, Black Men and the Police by Obasi Okorie, Ekemini Hogan and Utibe Effiong (October 14, 2020); 4.1 Teaching About Racism Is Essential for Education by the Editors of *Scientific American* (February 1, 2022); 4.2 Where Are the Black Women in STEM Leadership? by Erika Jefferson (April 23, 2019); 4.3 This Is What the Race Gap in Academia Looks Like by Amanda Montañez (February 19, 2018); 4.4 The Brilliance Paradox: What Really Keeps Women and Minorities from Excelling in Academia by Andrei Cimpian and Sarah-Jane Leslie (September 1, 2017); 5.1 Silence Is Never Neutral; Neither Is Science by 500 Women Scientists Leadership (June 6, 2020); 5.2 How to Study Racial Disparities by Bryan Schonfeld and Sam Winter-Levy (August 14, 2020); 5.3 Black Images Matter: How Cameras Helped, and Sometimes Harmed, Black People by Ainissa G. Ramirez (July 8, 2020); 5.4 The Racist Legacy of Computer-Generated Humans by Theodore Kim (August 18, 2020); 6.1 How to Unlearn Racism by Abigail Libers (October 1, 2020); 6.2 Charles Blow Tells You How to Actually Fight Racism by Bernadette Bynoe (March 19, 2021); 6.3 To Fight Bias, Consider Highlighting Your Race or Gender by Erika Kirgios, Aneesh Rai, Edward Chang and Katy Milkman (March 28, 2022); 6.4 We'll Never Fix Systemic Racism by Being Polite by Aldon Morris (August 3, 2020).

Each author biography was accurate at the time the article was originally published.

Content originally published on or after July 1, 2018, was reproduced with permission. Copyright © 2023 Scientific American, a Division of Springer Nature America, Inc. All rights reserved.

Content originally published from January 1, 2010, to June 30, 2018, was reproduced with permission. Copyright © 2023 Scientific American, a Division of Nature America, Inc. All rights reserved.

Content originally published on or before December 31, 2009, was reproduced with permission. Copyright © 2023 Scientific American, Inc. All rights reserved.

INDEX

A
Arbery, Ahmaud, 64, 129
asthma, 38, 41, 51, 86–88

B
Birth of a Nation, The, 121
Black Lives Matter movement, 5, 26, 54, 63, 82, 110, 112, 123, 129, 139, 141, 150, 151
Black Women in Science and Engineering (BWISE), 95–96
Blow, Charles, 139–145
"brilliance factor," and diversity in academia, 97–98, 99–107
Brown, Michael, 5, 26, 70, 82

C
Camden, N.J., police department, rebuilding of, 84
Campaign Zero, 82–83
Center for Policing Equity (CPE), 76–80
Cheddar Man, 10
community policing, 79, 84
computer-generated imagery, racist legacy of, 124–126
COVID-19 pandemic, 38, 39, 46, 48, 49–50, 57, 59–63, 65, 71, 75, 90, 91, 110, 112, 114, 115, 116, 118–119, 129, 137, 139–140, 151
critical race theory, 90–92
Critical Whiteness Studies (CWS), 132–133

D
de-escalation training, 81–85
Diallo, Amadou, 16–17
Douglass, Frederick, 120–123, 132
DuBois, W.E.B., 120–121, 132

E
explicit bias, 12, 16, 17–18, 19, 23, 78, 110, 134

F
Floyd, George, 26, 57, 64–65, 67, 70–71, 82, 112, 114, 123, 129, 140, 151

G
Garner, Eric, 5, 26, 86, 88
genetics, and the concept of "race," 5, 8–11, 131

Index

Glaser, Jack, 76–80
Great Migration, 121
Griffith, D. W., 121

H
hate crimes, 8, 12, 27
health care/physicians, and racial bias, 19, 20, 25, 38–50, 51–53, 59–63, 64–67, 71, 87, 140
Hoag, Alexis J., 71–75

I
Implicit Association Test (IAT), 23–24, 133
implicit bias, 12–22, 23–25, 26–27, 33, 66, 75, 76–80, 110, 133–136
implicit bias training, 76–80, 82, 130, 133–135

J
Jones, Camara Phyllis, 59–63, 66

K
King, Martin Luther, Jr., 35, 36, 150, 151, 152

L
Lacks, Henrietta, 111
Law Enforcement Action Partnership (LEAP), 84
Lewis, John Robert, 50

M
Martin, Trayvon, 26
mental health system, and racial bias, 54–58
microaggressions, 33–36, 66, 139

O
Obama, Barack, 5, 29, 31, 82

P
People's Institute for Survival and Beyond (PISAB), 128, 129, 134, 135, 136
police racism/violence, 5, 24, 30, 63, 70–75, 76–80, 81–85, 86–88, 114, 116, 151–152
post-treatment bias, 114–119
President's Task Force on 21st Century Policing, 81

R
Reagan, Ronald, 11

S
same-race memory advantage, 14
science institutions, and silence on racism, 110–113

T
Taylor, Breonna, 26, 65, 82, 129, 140

Till, Emmett, photographs of, 122, 123
Trump, Donald, 8, 73, 148, 150, 152
Tuskeegee Experiment, 111

W
"weapon bias," 17, 24
Wells, Ida B., 122